The Report from the Commission on Urban Life and Faith

Faithful Cities

A call for celebration, vision and justice

Methodist
Publishing House

CHURCH HOUSE
PUBLISHING

Contents

Methodist Publishing House
4 John Wesley Road
Peterborough
PE4 6ZP

Church House Publishing
Church House
Great Smith Street
London
SW1P 3NZ

1-85852-315-X

978-1-85852-315-6

Published 2006 by Methodist
Publishing House and Church
House Publishing

Designed by S2design and
advertising

Printed in England by Stanley
Hunt (printers) Ltd

Front cover
Main cover photo:
F8-infinity photography © 2005
Inset images left to right
(repeated on this page).
© Photodics Inc
© Ingram Publishing image library.
© Joy Douglas
© Photodics Inc.

Back cover inset images
left to right
© Joy Douglas
© Andy Stonehouse 2005
© David Johnston 2004

Foreword

This report is offered by the Commission on Urban Life and Faith with the intention of stimulating discussion and action among those whose lives are lived out in an urban setting and those to whom is given the responsibility for formulating policies that affect these lives.

The process through which we have passed in the last two years has been important to us. We have met and talked with hundreds of people in cities and towns. We have visited projects that have inspired and stimulated us and we are deeply indebted to those who have shared generously their insights, wisdom, visions and frustrations and helped us to understand more of the delights, injustices and needs of urban living. It is often at the local level that the language of love, hope, judgement, forgiveness, remembrance and hospitality combine to offer something tangible.

We are all too aware that this report is more 'work in progress' than a definitive conclusion to our activities and discussions. We have reflected on our experiences and offer our observations and some recommendations, but it is a changing scene, not least because of government initiatives and the renewed vigour among people of faith.

The recommendations we make rise out of the conviction that there is already much to be celebrated, that visions of a renewed citizenship have the potential for a society in which all flourish and that justice is the bedrock of well-being.

Beyond all this is the conviction that God is in the city and the kingdom of God is at hand.

Kathleen Richardson

The Revd Baroness Richardson of Calow,
Chair of the Commission on Urban Life and Faith

Introduction

Quite early on in this report you will find a chart setting out some of the things that have changed since the publication, twenty one years ago, of *Faith in the City* – and some of the things that haven't changed as well. It is a very instructive overview, which will help to explain some of the main directions and aspirations of this new contribution to thinking about our urban future.

The Commission that produced *Faith in the City* was faced with the task of alerting a public and a Government that seemed to be imperfectly aware of the impact of its policies upon the poorest in Britain to the urgency of public investment in combating urban destitution; and it also galvanized the Church into action, generating the Church Urban Fund, which has been one of the most effective and often (sadly) one of the least celebrated resources in urban regeneration over recent decades.

But the British city, like the rest of British and global society, has moved on. Urban redevelopment has transformed one landscape after another. Patterns of work and employment have altered radically. Ethnic and religious pluralism are far more evident; and the issues around religious plurality, not least (but not only) in relation to our British Muslim communities, have become more and more complex and pressing. In responding to destitution and disadvantage, the culture is one dominated by the model of partnership. The polarization often taken for granted two decades ago between state-generated solutions and private charity – always a gross over-simplification – has long faded away. It is no exaggeration to speak, as this report does, of a 'regeneration industry'.

Yet the questions to be asked are as sharp and uncomfortable as they were in 1985. What drives regeneration – the actual needs of communities or the agenda of developers? What messages are given by the quality and character of the built environment? Are we creating new kinds of exclusion by building policies that reduce the social mix of an area? And, very importantly, how do we change the hectic atmosphere of much regeneration work, harried by rapidly changing and highly complicated government requirements and dominated by short-term and sometimes superficial or cosmetic goals? How do we create partnerships that can find their own appropriate pace for development and their own appropriate levels of accountability, in a way that will leave communities with an enhanced sense of their resources and capacities? Too often at present, as the report

spells out, the reality is of deeply frustrated workers, trying to juggle immensely complex demands and left after three years with projects half-realized and local hopes disappointed.

This is where the central idea of the report comes in: 'faithful capital'. While admitting the slightly doubtful aura that hangs around the word 'capital' in this context, the writers argue that the Church represents a resource which is bound to think in terms of sustained commitment. Its fundamental beliefs are about such commitment – God's commitment to a people, Christ's commitment to a weak and failing body of human followers, the commitment embodied (literally) in incarnation and resurrection. The question the Church always has to ask of any society, and any project within society, is about how it reflects the kind of enduring commitment to individuals and groups that builds them up and changes them and makes them what they can be. In other words, the deeper issues around regeneration and development that are raised in this report are to do with how our corporate life shows something of what God is like and thus something of what humanity, made in God's image, might be.

The resources of 'faith communities', now so significant in public thinking about regeneration and the fight against disadvantage, are not just a matter of assorted and ill-defined moral values; they are to do with what sort of God is believed in and what awkward questions are made possible by such a God. The specific contribution from the Judeo-Christian tradition is to point to a God who is above all characterized by faithfulness. It is God's faithfulness that is the most profound resource for all our life together as human beings. And the challenge that this report puts before us is how we who live out of that eternal faithfulness can keep faith with our neighbours.

It is a challenge we need to hear, and we should be profoundly grateful to the writers of this report for setting it before us with such a wealth of narrative, analysis and vision; grateful also to all those who, by using 'faithful capital' in all the varied contexts of urban life today, have begun to show us what is possible for our society. I hope that these pages will prompt as radical and long-lasting a response, in Church and society, as did *Faith in the City* in its day.

Dr Rowan Williams,
Archbishop of Canterbury

1 Faithful Cities:
Places of Celebration, Vision and Justice

A view from the London Eye　[B1.1]

Imagine that you are taking your nephew or niece for a ride on the giant ferris wheel on the bank of the Thames, the London Eye, and using the occasion to say something about the structures of society. The first thing you both see are the great buildings of Westminster and Whitehall. These, you say, are the homes of government, and government is about the concentration and distribution of power. Next you see shops and offices, and in the distance the Stock Exchange. These, you explain, are the home of the market, and the market is about the production and distribution of wealth. Then your nephew or niece notices the dome of St Paul's and the various church spires still visible between the tower blocks and asks, 'What are those?' You explain that they are houses of worship. 'And what,' he or she asks, 'do they produce and distribute?' Our first inclination might be to say that they are not that sort of place at all. This, I want to suggest, would be an error, but no mere error. In a certain sense it is a defining error of our culture.[1]
Dr Jonathan Sacks

1.1　What is it that makes our towns and cities flourish? In the words of the question that has animated this Commission throughout its deliberations, 'What makes a good city?' This is essentially what Jonathan Sacks is asking – what criteria do we use to judge its most significant qualities?

1.2　Clearly politics and economics are fundamental but when it comes to identifying the wellsprings of a society's core values – what Sacks calls its 'moral sense' – we need to consider other, less tangible, dimensions. Chief among these are the contributions made to the common good by religious faith. In fact, in this report we claim that there is something which we call 'faithful capital' – a quality related to 'social capital' (a term in common currency among urban commentators). Faithful capital is something that can be found in abundance in the congregations and communities of faith and is – we will argue – crucial to the survival and sustenance of urban life.

1.3　Faith is still vibrant, diverse and alive in the city. As Jonathan Sacks lyrically observes, you can see the signs of it when you scan the skyscape of any of our cities. But this faith is not just signalled in church spires, in the domes and pillars of mosques, synagogues, temples and gurdwaras. It is also powerfully present in the hearts and minds of millions of twenty-first-century citizens and, springing from those faithful lives, it is present too in the countless daily actions inspired by religious hope, belief and obligation.

1.4　Twenty years ago, when *Faith in the City*, the report of the Archbishop's Commission on Urban Priority Areas was published, media pundits could have been excused if they had predicted a very different picture. Conventional wisdom suggested a gradual but irreversible dwindling in the profile and influence of religion in our towns and cities. And while Sunday church attendance has fallen steadily until recently, that is in part because the story of faith in twenty-first-century urban Britain is being transformed.

1.5　Our two-year-long study has found that faith is now a more dynamic and significant factor in our cities than it was 20 years ago. Not only has the Church

Urban Fund, which sprang from the *Faith in the City* report, catalysed Christian engagement in our urban centres, but now there is a broader contribution, for instance of Hindu, Muslim and Sikh communities, than previously. And today the Government recognizes the uniquely significant role of faith communities in social cohesion, education and regeneration. But the organized religion of the major historic faiths does not monopolize issues of faith and spirituality. There is now a wider, less coherent, assent among British people that our world is more than matter.

1.6   The language of 'spirituality' is often associated with what sociologists have called 'self-religions', characterized by personal quests for meaning or with the pursuit of 'New Age' therapies and techniques. While not denying the virtue or authenticity of such explorations, that is not the territory we map in this report.

1.7   We are talking about a spirituality which, while universal, is specifically and historically expressed in the major world faiths. At its most basic level, this is a vision of reality that goes beyond the material and the physical – our human experience is part of something larger than itself. And because our common origins are in God we have a connectedness with all other created beings, including nature. And it is our task to sustain and enhance life for all.

1.8   Clearly, all these faith traditions are diverse within themselves as well as in relation to one another, with points of difference as well as convergence in their teachings. Yet they share core principles and convictions from which this common 'moral sense' – which informs faithful capital – emerges. What we glimpse through the inherited wisdom of our faith traditions lies at the heart of our lives together as communities and people of faith, and it constitutes the essence of the insights we offer in this report.

1.9   What we have to say grows out of three key convictions: about what we understand about the nature of God; about what it means to be human; and about how humanity should live in community together.

1.10   First, we understand God to be source of all life from whom all creation draws its purpose and character. Secondly, we understand that to be human means that we are made 'in the image and likeness of God', and that therefore each person possesses an innate and irreducible dignity. Thirdly, our traditions speak of humanity being called into relationship with God and that human purpose and destiny is fulfilled in relationships of mutuality, love and justice.

Discovering faithful capital

1.11   It follows, then, that the quality of our life in community – secular and religious – should be an outworking of this model of human and divine in relationship. Our 'moral sense' of society tells us that *life itself* is sacred, that our *individual lives* are interconnected and our *common life* should be constructed to enable all people to flourish. This is the wellspring of faithful capital.

1.12   One of the most powerful gifts that faith-based organizations have to offer is that they are instructed to 'practise what they preach'. A commitment to human flourishing and a vision of the good city can therefore never simply remain at the level of doctrine or abstract principles – it finds its expression in a myriad of locally based, grassroots activity – what Leonie Sandercock calls 'a thousand tiny empowerments'[2] – that seek to make a difference.

1.13   Herein lies the notion of faithful capital. There is already a growing familiarity with the idea of 'social capital'. This term describes the way that people are enriched not only by their ownership of physical and financial assets or by the 'human capital' of their skills and qualifications, but also by their social relationships and participation in social networks. Sociologist John Field sums it up in two words, 'relationships matter'. He continues: 'By making connections with one another, and keeping them going over time, people are able to work together to achieve things that they either could not achieve by themselves, or could only achieve with great difficulty. People connect through a series of networks and they tend to share common values with other members of these networks; to the extent that these networks constitute a resource, they can be seen as forming a kind of capital.'[3]

1.14   This emphasis on human relationships and connections holds an immediate attraction, not least for Christians. The development of social capital also seems very significant in attempts to build the connections and trust necessary for living together in a diverse community and society.

1.15   It has to be said that social capital is the subject of keen debate and criticism. Some see the language of 'capital' as reducing human relationships to an instrumental currency and as being bound to governmental economic and social calculations, priorities and policies. Many (not least faith and community participants in regeneration) question this. And, of course, not all social networks and the stocks of social capital that they harbour are benign – including religion itself.

1.16   Nevertheless, we see 'social capital' as an essentially helpful idea. And we suggest that, at their best, churches and Christians – alongside congregations of other faiths and their adherents – offer a particular gift to communities. We have chosen to call this gift 'faithful capital'.[4] In corporate and personal worship, prayer, reading and meditation there is regular and explicit reminder and celebration of the gift of life and recognition and remembrance of guilt, forgiveness and healing. This inspires the commitment to personal and collective transformation, love for neighbour and care for 'the stranger', and to human dignity and social justice. Genuinely distinctive and important contributions to wider social capital are made when this faith is acted out in the wider community in authentic local engagement. Two particular distinguishing elements of faithful capital are its *language* and its *practices*.

1.17   The language of 'love', 'hope', 'judgement', 'forgiveness', 'remembrance' and 'hospitality' combine to form a distinctive 'story'. The very meaning of 'regeneration' (a word with strong religious roots) is given a deeper spiritual and social significance that challenges dominant definitions in public policy.

1.18   Similarly, the practical ways of working of many churches and other local congregations is often distinctive. Although there has been a growth in the number of 'churches of choice', which draw people from long distances, there are still many 'churches of place' with strong local connections. This local rootedness is often very longstanding, encouraging a commitment to people that is tolerant of slow progress and assigns importance to particular relationships and the needs of specific people and groups. In research funded by the Joseph Rowntree Foundation, people of faith spoke of the importance of recognizing and accepting fallibility and failure and of responding with patience and perseverance – given hope by their belief in ultimate love, justice and reconciliation.[5] A further widely held value emerged in research by the William Temple Foundation, which identified genuine participation and working together with other organizations as an essential element of faithful capital.[6]

1.19   From a governmental point of view, the social capital and, specifically, the faithful capital offered by Christian churches and other faith organizations can be seen as both a valuable resource and as a source of discomfiture. Commitment to neighbourhood, long-term presence, strong value base, important community facilities, bridging inter-faith networks – they all offer paths to the grails of 'community cohesion' and urban 'regeneration'. On the other hand, the distinct and conflicting language of faith, the values that challenge rather than support government policy, and working styles that fail to mesh with time-limited, benchmark-driven outcome-required government schemes, all pose a challenge.

1.20   We are not saying that only people or communities of faith have anything to offer in the making of good cities. We pay tribute to the thousands of people who would not claim – and in some cases would shun – association with religion or faith, yet who selflessly work for the common good. We also want to recognize that there are many people of faith who choose to put their talents and energy at the disposal of secular organizations and institutions, rather than through specifically religious initiatives. It is all to the good.

1.21 If the notion of faithful capital is the 'Big Idea' at the heart of this report, it is not the only one. However, almost all the other major planks of the report are associated with this core theme.

1.22 Fundamental to faithful capital, for instance is the very presence of people and communities of faith in our country's most deprived urban areas. The Church of England, in particular, because of its parish system, has buildings and networks of people given over to the long-term service of its geographical neighbours, regardless of the volatile chemistry of demography and property values. Not only are faith communities in cities physically present, they are actively, dutifully and often passionately engaged in caring for those who need care most.

1.23 In our ethnically and socially diverse cities – where fear of 'the other' stalks the streets, and where both rich and poor are tempted to ghettoize – conventional wisdom calls for a spirit of tolerance. The faithful, at best, reject this passive and paternalistic entreaty, calling instead for acts of hospitality – extending beyond the usual boundaries of nationality, race, creed, gender or class – drawn from ancient traditions which demand a welcome for the stranger.

1.24 Faithfulness demands a critical rather than a docile partnership with the agencies of regeneration and development – be they government or commercial. This means that some fundamental questions need to be asked about the criteria for successful urban redevelopment. Individual prosperity, growth and land value are not sufficient on their own. Happiness, well-being and public space, for example, all need to be accounted for and valued. All these make for a good city.

1.25 The experience of the faithful on the ground is that the poor – if not getting quantifiably poorer – are the losers in a widening gulf between themselves and those who were growing more prosperous. There is a supreme irony in the way that when redevelopment and regeneration take place, too often it is people experiencing poverty who are moved or stranded. Scandalously, we live in one of the most unequal countries in Europe,[7] where the 'trickle down' promise of market forces has failed to deliver, and where a draconian asylum system consigns a small section of the population to unacceptable destitution.

1.26 This report is committed to empowerment and participation, grounded in a vision of human dignity and equal value. The Commission found that many visions of the good city depend on the 'top-down' imposition of values and projects. But if the dominant idea of much urban regeneration is one of 'delivering a good city to the people', then faith traditions offer alternative understandings. In the Hebrew Scriptures, when the people of Israel were instructed to build a 'tabernacle' or place of divine dwelling, they were instructed both to make it portable and to ensure that its construction reflected the labour and gifts of the people (Exodus 26). This serves as a reminder that the divine never has a final resting-place – the labours of the people have a role in building the sacred as well as the profane. Cities, as human dwelling places which somehow prefigure and point to the presence of God within them, are always 'under construction', and need the active and continuing participation of all parts of the community to fulfil their potential.

1.27 In geographer Doreen Massey's words, 'the making of the city goes on'.[8] Our contemporary cities are also always under construction – we celebrate the vitality and dynamism of cities and their ability to receive and integrate the offerings of newcomers as well as their established members.

1.28 In this report, we argue that despite its ambivalent history, and its capacity to incite hatred and conflict, religious faith is still one of the richest, most enduring and most dynamic sources of energy and hope for cities. Faith is a vital – and often essential – resource in the building of relationships, and communities. In the values they promote, in the service they inspire, and in the resources they command, faith-based organizations make a decisive difference to their communities. So we return to Jonathan Sacks' illustration of the 'bird's-eye view' of London, and affirm with him the significance of a 'spiritual dimension' to our evaluation of urban life and faith.

Summary of chapters

1.29   We begin in Chapters 2 and 3 by addressing the dramatic change in the nature of urban life over the past 20 years. In Chapter 2, we review the impact of *Faith in the City* (the report of the Archbishop's Commission on Urban Priority Areas) since it was published 20 years ago, in 1985. Enormously influential and controversial in its day, its trenchant criticism of government policy and its recommendations left a vital legacy. We examine that legacy and outline our response to the new urban vista of the twenty-first century.

1.30   One dramatic change in 20 years, as Chapter 3 indicates, is the huge amount of religious and cultural diversity in our major cities and towns. Globalization has brought ambiguities and fears as well as riches and opportunities with this diversity. This can, and has, bred hostility and the advent of rejectionist, 'furious religion',[9] together with new expressions of racism and xenophobia.

1.31   There is a danger that as cities become more diverse, so different communities co-exist in parallel with no points of contact or common ground. Often we experience our neighbours as strangers. Chapter 3 therefore asks if religious faith, far from being a divisive force, can be a source of solidarity and cohesion – turning 'strangers' into 'neighbours' through proactive hospitality.

1.32   Chapter 4 traces the new map of poverty and prosperity and concludes that, once again, the values of faith have a positive potential. Even living in the lap of prosperity we find an impoverishment in people's sense of well-being. As the Government strives to tackle the inequalities in our society, it has to face the fact that economic indicators alone are inadequate reflections of social and personal prosperity, and find more inclusive measures that reflect people's deeper needs.

1.33   Levels of debt, the correlation between poverty and other measures of deprivation, such as poor health, vulnerability to crime and low educational attainment are an urgent matter of conscience. So too is the gulf between the values of urban communities themselves and those who seek purely economic solutions upon them.

1.34   In Chapter 5, therefore, we hear some of the stories of those who challenge the shortcomings of an overemphasis on status, power and profit. We dig deeper into the disjunction between the official aspirations of regeneration and their real impact, and discover that the rhetoric frequently falls short of reality.

1.35   This points to some questions: for whose benefit is regeneration? And who represents the long-term interests of local communities if they are at odds with the 'short-termist', target-driven culture of the regeneration industry? We chart how faith-based organizations and their coalitions are ideally placed to take on such a representative role and mobilize their communities around common interests.

1.36   Chapter 6 looks at the way cities have developed over the centuries and then moves to a more extended reflection on some of the values and perspectives that might inform processes of growth and regeneration. What constitutes a sustainable and just urban society, and what might be the continuing role of the churches and other faith traditions?

1.37   'What makes a good city?' has been a key question for the Commissioners. By asking this simple question in our seminars, meetings and visits we have been able to dig deeper into the underlying values informing many of the most ambitious programmes of regeneration currently under way in our major cities – not only in the UK, but internationally.

1.38   As Chapter 6 argues, strategies for regeneration frequently coalesce around four key principles of a good or successful city: (1) economics, (2) environment and infrastructure, (3) politics and governance and (4) culture. These four 'pillars of regeneration' relate to questions of physical resources, wealth-creation, sustainability and political structures. What they don't do is to take into account less quantifiable questions such as quality of life, well-being, happiness even – what we might term the 'human face' of the city. We have to ask questions about the *soul* of the city as well, and about how faith communities can help develop this.

1.39   Chapter 7 examines some of the dilemmas facing faith-based organizations that enter into partnerships with local government in various projects of neighbourhood renewal, provision of services, capacity building and community development. The chapter argues that such concern for the well-being of the society is rooted in a radically inclusive vision of human flourishing and is something to be shared across the boundaries of faith. It identifies the beginnings of a 'public theology' of involvement that draws upon the core principles of hospitality, communion and incarnation.

1.40   Yet it is also important to ask whether faith-based organizations' involvement with various regeneration programmes has resulted in a distortion of their own priorities. Is it possible for faith groups to construct partnerships that deliver real regeneration and without simply being co-opted by those in power?

1.41   Chapter 8 celebrates the dogged and heroic presence of congregations in beleaguered urban areas and asks about the cost of such involvement on often quite fragile embattled communities, and what needs to be done to equip, support and sustain them. Just as *Faith in the City* addressed the question of resourcing Urban Priority churches in the service of their local communities, therefore, so we will be concerned to ask what kinds of 'capacity building' are necessary for the long-term effectiveness of faith-based organizations.

1.42   We are realistic about the state of our cities and urban areas, but we are not gloomy. We celebrate the diversity, the ebb and flow of change and the way that the global becomes local, and personal. And we have a vision of the good city rooted in the love, determination and the uncompromising call for justice and peace that arises from faithful capital. This is a city which is continually being built.

2.1   Our work as a Commission has not taken place in a historical vacuum. As well as offering a vision of twenty-first-century urban society and the Church's role within it, our work marks the twentieth anniversary of *Faith in the City*, the report of the Archbishop's Commission on Urban Priority Areas. The Commission on Urban Life and Faith therefore continues this active concern for urban society.

2.2   Twenty years on, we see both continuity and change. We recognize the enduring impact of *Faith in the City*. The 1985 report asked: What are the chief features of the 'delights, injustices and needs' facing our cities today? We pose the same question in a new urban context, and ask what challenges and opportunities these raise – for Church and nation, for communities and faith-communities.

Faith in the City: **Then and now**

2.3   The original Commission behind *Faith in the City* was established amid rising concern at the plight of many inner cities and outer council estates. In highlighting the growing number of neighbourhoods – or 'urban priority areas' – afflicted by economic decline, social disintegration and environmental decay, it laid the foundation for the Church of England's strategy for urban mission and ministry.

2.4   *Faith in the City* produced a series of recommendations: 33 to the Church of England and 26 to the nation at large. It called on the Government:

- For increases in social security benefits and greater expenditure on the youth service, training and job-creation;
- To invest significantly in public housing;
- To encourage community development and participation in local authority urban strategies;
- To address the problems of institutional racism in legal, criminal and public sectors.

2.5   To the Church it said:

- Resources should be diverted preferentially to parishes in urban priority areas (UPAs);
- Churches should be given the opportunity to undertake audits in order to review their priorities;
- More people from UPAs should be selected for ministerial training;
- Extended urban placements should become a central part of training for ordination.
- A caucus for Black Anglican concerns should be established.
- A 'Church Urban Fund' should be set up to provide financial support for local community projects.

2.6   *Faith in the City* left two enduring legacies that have shaped the principles by which we have conducted our enquiries and the values informing our recommendations.

2.7   First, *Faith in the City* affirmed the Church's continuing presence in marginalized communities at a time when many other agencies were abandoning urban priority areas.

2.8   Twenty years ago, the Commissioners made a point of visiting many of these places, believing that such first-hand experience of urban life was essential to their enquiries. This signalled a strong commitment to listening to the experiences of ordinary people, and to valuing voices and perspectives not normally heard in the public domain.

'It was powerful and passionate; it was far removed from the traditional parody of the Church of England as the Tory party at prayer.'
Peter Hall, *Cities of Tomorrow* [1]

'It is about the repentance and rebirth of the Church of England, it is also about the overall political and human integrity of our society.'
Anthony Dyson, Review of *Faith in the City* [2]

'It seems likely that . . . the two most significant events in English church history in the 1980s will be the Pope's visit to Canterbury and the publication of *Faith in the City*.'
Adrian Hastings, *A History of English Christianity* [3]

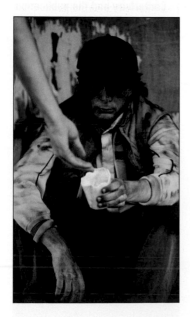

2.9   A conviction that the state of our cities acts as a vital litmus test of how much we can call ourselves a just and equitable society has also been central to our commission.

2.10   A wholehearted commitment to the city is rooted in our understanding of the nature of God, humanity and the world. In the Christian tradition, cities are central to human civilization, an essential part of the human story and the continuing story of those who follow in the footsteps of Christ. This conviction springs from an 'incarnational' theology – a conviction that by sending his Son Jesus, God shares in and affirms our human condition. Christians also believe that Jesus identified closely with those who were poor and excluded – and so it is in the voices and struggles of the poor that we can recognize the face of Christ today.

2.11   *Faith in the City* saw something about the nature of God's love for humanity and God's care for the poor in the stories emerging from the experiences and voices of ordinary people. We have also sought to give voice to a 'contextual theology' that celebrates the city, and identifies signs of hope and resurrection in ordinary urban life and faith – often beyond the boundaries of institutional Christianity.

2.12   The second enduring legacy of *Faith in the City* is more paradoxical. The report's political impact lay in its ability to synthesize and give voice to a huge amount of dissatisfaction with the Government of the day. It spoke out on behalf of marginalized communities against what many perceived as a heartless and unhearing Government. It also focused explicitly on the plight of the poorest of the poor in some of the most neglected and under-resourced areas of the country.

2.13   Some argue this was because *Faith in the City* embraced liberation theology's doctrine of God's 'preferential option for the poor'. But the reality may have been far more prosaic. Such a strong identification with urban priority areas was primarily rooted in the parish system, which places the Church in every part of the land. With that presence comes an enduring responsibility to minister for the whole population of a parish – not just those who turn up at services.

2.14   This meant that the Church retained a presence in some of the most marginalized communities at a time when many agencies were withdrawing. It also meant that the Church could call on a range of skills and resources – including paid ministers, congregations, volunteers, skills, buildings – which could be placed at the disposal of local people and organizations.

2.15   The original Commission regarded its report as upholding 'those basic Christian principles of justice and compassion which we believe we share with the great majority of the people of Britain'. This reflected an assumption that the Church of England was capable of speaking on behalf of the nation at large, acting almost as the 'conscience of the nation'. Such a presumption to speak on behalf of a wider 'common good' that transcended party politics was one of the factors at the root of government antipathy to the report. In the absence of more formal political alternatives, the report was cast as the mouthpiece of political opposition to Conservative policies.

2.16   But two decades later, this notion that the Church has the right to speak about anything on anyone's behalf is now open to question. Indeed, the changing nature and public influence of all the Christian denominations constitutes one of the most striking changes between the era of *Faith in the City* and our own.

Then and now: a sketch of how we were and how we are

1985	2006
Increasing global competition – liberalization of financial markets	Accelerated economic globalization sustained by the 'net society'
High inflation/high unemployment; deindustrialization	Low inflation/lower unemployment; growing dominance of the service sector
Anti-union legislation, defeat of miners' strike	Contraction of unions, 'flexible' labour force – work insecurity and pension concerns extend to non-manual workers: transfer of risk to the individual
Increasing working hours related to changing employment conditions	Work-life balance concerns (cash-rich/time-poor)
North/south divide – spatial polarization at urban and regional levels	Dominance of London and the South-East underlined; changing patterns of spatial polarization
Concern about 'poverty'	Concern about 'social exclusion'
Substantial social housing stock	Owner-occupation dominant
Cold War – threat of conflict involving nation states and alliances	Collapse of Communism; tension between the West and Muslim world; threat of conflict involving terrorism
Apartheid in South Africa	Democratic multi-ethnic South Africa
Global inequality – famine, war, environmental degradation; growing debts in the South	Global inequality – famine, war, environmental degradation; pressure to cancel debt
Global inequality – famine, war, environmental degradation	Some debts cancelled
Influence of world institutions (UN, IMF, World Bank etc.)	American unilateralism challenged by anti-capitalist alliances and new social movements
'Thatcherism' (combining liberal economics and social conservatism)	New Labour and the 'Third Way' – changes and continuities in policy
Politics of production	Politics of consumption and identity
Political centralization in Britain	Contradictory developments – central regulation devolution and localism
Emphasis still on representative democracy but with growing range of non-elected quangos	Decline in voter turnout; shift from municipal government to a more fragmented governance; the rise of 'partnerships'
Mainly national media – prominence of the BBC/ 'public broadcasting'	Global media – multi-channel TV and new media
Growing social diversity – campaigns by women, gay people and people with disabilities	Accelerated social diversity – more (although still incomplete) recognition of minority rights of women and minorites
Ethnic inequality Racism – focus on immigration and urban 'riots' (post-Scarman Report)	Continuing ethnic inequality and racism Racism – post-Stephen Lawrence Inquiry acceptance of 'institutional racism'. Asylum a growing political and social issue
Increasing working hours related to changing employment conditions	'Work-life balance' concerns – long working hours (cash-rich/time-poor)
Growing distrust of expects and the authority of the producer'	The 'authority of the consumer' and the significance of local experience
Church-state tension; pressure to define religion as private	State interest in enlisting 'faith communities' in public policy
Rise of world fundamentalisms as a challenge to modernity	Post-September 11 – association of religion with division
Anglican Communion divided on women's ordination	Anglican Communion divided on homosexuality
Church of England clergy remain all-male	Ordination of women to the Church of England priesthood from 1994
Denominational boundaries continue after Covenanting-for-Unity scheme rejected in 1992	Anglican-Methodist Covenant moves forward
Limited inter-faith dialogue	Growing inter-faith dialogue

2.17   British society has been transformed over the past 20 years. There have been great improvements in the UK's economic performance and in many people's living standards:

- A series of government initiatives, starting with the renewal of the physical fabric of inner-city areas under the Conservatives in the 1980s, through the introduction of *City Challenge* in 1991 and programmes such as Single Regeneration Budgets, New Deal for Communities and the Neighbourhood Renewal Fund, have injected significant levels of funding into urban areas.
- The election of the Labour Government in 1997 heralded a more deliberate approach to tackling poverty and social exclusion, including the introduction of a minimum wage.
- Unemployment is at its lowest rate for around 30 years.

2.18   While Government policies have reduced poverty and stimulated economic growth, in other respects, the picture is less promising. Marked poverty and inequality persists, despite record levels of employment and nearly a decade of consistent economic growth. And as Professor Richard Wilkinson points out in his book *The Impact of Inequality*,[6] however prosperous a country, if there is a yawning gap between rich and poor, there is a corrosive effect on society. Income poverty has increased during the 1980s and 1990s: from 13% in 1979, to 25% in 1996–97 and 21% in 2003–04.

2.19   Poverty also disproportionately affects members of the Black and ethnic minority communities, people with disabilities or long-term illnesses, older people, families with children and those in major urban centres.

2.20   Against this backdrop, the seismic economic changes that took place during the 1980s continue to have an impact, most particularly in the shape of the long-term decline of heavy manufacturing industries and the emergence of retail, service and information-based jobs.

2.21   Perhaps the single most significant new development in the last 20 years – and one which constitutes a significant thread in our reflections – is the extent to which cities have been transformed through economic and environmental regeneration. Our major cities are now no longer abandoned husks of post-industrial decay, but hubs of vibrant economic and cultural activity – often focused on city centres and river and dockland redevelopment. Nevertheless, there often remains a great gulf between those with enough money to take advantage of new entertainment, retailing, leisure and accommodation complexes, and those without.

2.22   In other respects, too, the scale of economic factors has changed in ways unforeseen in 1985. Chief among these must be the impact of 'globalization'.

2.23   Globalization means people migrate to find work, making the population of cities more ethnically diverse and cosmopolitan. A number of mega-cities have grown up, such as Tokyo, Los Angeles, Mexico City and London, which dominate their regional and national economies. Tourism, the leisure industry and travel have expanded, favouring urban conurbations with good transport infrastructure.[8] Increasing dependence on the international flow of investment means that local economies often stand or fall by business decisions made on the other side of the world.

2.24   With ethnic diversity has come renewed attention to issues of immigration, nationality and citizenship. A generation ago, debates about race relations and immigration centred on the rights of British citizens from the former Commonwealth countries in South Asia, Africa and the Caribbean. Today, political attention – and controversy – focuses on the status of migrants, often from eastern Europe, the Middle East or Africa.

2.25   Reignited anxieties about immigration have been exploited by extremist groups who exercise a malign influence over many of our most disadvantaged urban communities. This takes place on both sides of the ethnic coin. For instance, we see the 'white supremacy' of the British National Party (BNP) on the one hand, and on the other an 'Islamic rejectionism' which turns its back on the experience of diversity.

2.26   The advent of greater ethnic diversity in our cities brings with it greater religious pluralism. A complex and often contradictory picture emerges.

2.27   The numerical decline of organized religion continues – most acutely affecting mainstream Christian denominations. Yet, at the same time, in the 2001 Census over 70% of those expressing a faith commitment identify themselves as 'Christian' – but without any formal affiliation to organized religion.

2.28   As the high tide of formal, institutional Christianity recedes, it reveals a more complex and differentiated picture. Faith communities in urban areas are increasingly ethnically, socially and culturally very diverse. We see a shift in the composition of inner-city congregations. Older, traditional ways of being church are being superseded by new, eclectic – often evangelical or Pentecostal – churches. Within this mix, socially active Black majority congregations are developing prominence in inner cities and becoming a voice in urban civil society.

2.29   Similarly, the growth of urban populations with allegiances to Islam, Hinduism and Sikhism means a new resurgent presence of faith-based communities that are increasingly active in community development, education and local politics.

2.30   This, too, gives a global character to the nature of faith and identity. British Muslims, Sikhs and Hindus, while happily identifying themselves as UK citizens, nevertheless often also have family and national loyalties beyond these shores. This affects people's political sympathies, for instance, over the allied occupation of Iraq.

2.31   Such proliferation of manifestations of faith is not restricted to organized religion. It can also be seen in people's enduring interest in 'spirituality' – anything from cathedral services to a search for 'sacred space' in crowded cities.

2.32   In 1985, *Faith in the City* referred to 'the arrival in our cities of large numbers of adherents of other faiths', but did not anticipate the implications of cultural and religious pluralism or the role of a broad range of faith communities.

2.33   In contrast, this Commission is keenly aware that our analysis of urban life and faith must reflect, and respond to, this greater diversity. We argue that not only the churches, but all people of faith, are engaging with urban society. This is manifest in countless examples of action which counter and transcend the fragmentation, impoverishment and despair that still haunt our cities. For this reason, from the beginning our Commission included people from a wide range of Christian denominations and from Islamic and Jewish perspectives.

Faith in the public agenda

2.34   Faith and religion have become increasingly prominent in the debate about urban regeneration over the past 20 years – especially since the election of the New Labour Government in 1997. All levels of government have recognized the contribution of so called 'faith communities' to urban regeneration. Efforts have been made to include faith-based organizations in many initiatives – a considerable gain since *Faith in the City*.

2.35   The Urban White Paper, *Our Towns and Cities – The Future*,[9] for example, published in 2000, identified faith communities as a crucial means by which a broad cross-section of a local community might participate in regeneration. In the same year, the centre-left think tank Demos talked of the 'new covenant' between government and faith-based agencies. They noted that the latter had often been responsible for innovative projects in areas such as primary health care, homelessness, community regeneration and drug-related services. In particular, Demos observed such agencies 'taking account of the full range of human needs when providing care'.[10]

2.36   Similarly, in 2002, the Local Government Association drew up a guide for local authorities on how to include faith-based groups in neighbourhood renewal. That initiative in turn rested on a body known as the Inner Cities

'Manufacturing in the Black Country has been hit disproportionately, especially by the rise in sterling. Over the post-war period, the share of manufacturing in total output has fallen from over a third to around a fifth. Much of this decline is structural, the result of changes in demand and in the optimum location of business investment and activity around the world. It reflects the underlying shift in activity from the "old" to the "new" economies. The contraction of old industries is a consequence of the need for labour and capital to move into the expanding new industries. Although the output of the metal manufacturing and textile industries in the UK has fallen by around a third over the past thirty years, chemicals output has risen by some 140%. Even within engineering, traditional sectors such as metal manufacturing and machine tools have declined, and new sectors such as telecommunications have grown rapidly.

Manufacturing has also been more volatile than the economy as a whole. Since the beginning of 1993, manufacturing output rose at an average rate of 1.5% a year, about half that of the wider economy. Manufacturing has grown, but only an annual average of 0.6%, compared with growth in the whole economy of 2.6%. The problem facing many manufacturers is that output prices and hence profit margins, are too low relative to the costs of their inputs.'
Black Country Urban and Industrial Mission submission to CULF, 2005

Religious Council which, since 1994, has been deployed more actively in the Government's attempts to tackle urban renewal and social exclusion. In the north-west, two reports were published in 2003 and 2005 tracing the considerable 'added-value' contribution of faith-based organizations to many aspects of civil society (generating an estimated £95 million a year for the regional economy).

2.37 As a result of such active involvement by faith communities, observers have begun to see that faith-based groups have the potential to make a vital, unique contribution to the stock of social capital in any community.

2.38 Robert Putnam's book *Bowling Alone*,[11] exploring the fragmentation of civil society, was an early herald of this idea. The idea of social capital includes a whole range of activities and resources that build the bonds of social cohesion, active citizenship and democratic participation. All these contribute to a healthy civil society and a healthy city.

2.39 Religion and religious organizations could be said to be rich in social capital. They often have strong historical associations with a geographical place, and their buildings are often available for other people's activities as well as their own. Religion is good at 'networking' too – local congregations are linked to city-wide and even international faith traditions. Religion often brings strong traditions of social justice, with values of altruism and public service, which bear fruit in all sorts of community activities.

2.40 A study carried out in 2004 by Aston Business School[12] into the involvement of local parishes in the Diocese of Birmingham in their communities provides convincing evidence of their positive contribution to civil renewal. The kinds of projects these parishes initiated demonstrate a diversity of activities, reflecting a wide range of styles of engagement in community. Among other things, they:

- Employed and managed specialist development workers within the local community;
- Sponsored and co-ordinated externally funded projects such as community cafés, IT projects and credit unions;
- Provided rented meeting space for youth groups, adult education classes and advice surgeries;
- Organized luncheon clubs, playgroups and other services for the community.

2.41 The Aston report echoes similar research into the role of faith-based organizations by bodies such as the Northwest Regional Development Agency (see Chapter 8) by noting that one of the reasons they are effective is because local churches are able to draw in many of the core elements of social capital. This includes a reserve of skilled and highly committed volunteers, good organization and leadership, strong core values of partnership and inclusivity, stability and continuity, as well as basic resources such as buildings.

2.42 This model of religion as social capital sees faith communities harnessing values, resources and expertise for the encouragement of active citizenship and neighbourhood renewal. Representatives of Sheffield City Council, addressing a seminar in Manchester for CULF in July 2004, put it like this:

Clearly there are many examples of the faith community working in deprived neighbourhoods. Faith communities provide one of the strongest components of community cohesion, giving their adherents a sense of common identity beyond their immediate family and not based on social status or consumption. In the most difficult times and the hardest hit neighbourhoods they have kept alive people's dignity and hopes for something better.

2.43 At the heart of ideas of religion as 'social capital' is the notion that faith can be a source of shared moral values which are at the heart of strong communities. Philosophically, this goes deeper than a simple endorsement of religious groupings' 'involvement in community' as service providers. The argument is that strong values of how we live together in community are themselves integral to the regeneration of neighbourhoods and to society as a whole. Communities embody the very cultural and moral virtues that need to be revitalized if society is to tackle problems of poverty and social exclusion.

2.44   Government at local, regional and national level has woken up to the potential of faith-based organizations to make constructive contributions to their neighbourhoods. Many local authorities, in particular, see faith-based organizations as a way of getting access and delivering services to so-called 'hard-to-reach' groups. In practice, however, this often means 'religion' gets conflated with Black and ethnic minority communities in the minds of local authorities, with the result that their delivery of services and appreciation of religious and cultural diversity is confused.

2.45   Yet others will regard claims about the significance of 'faithful capital' as a way of religion making illegitimate inroads into the public domain. On the appointment of the Commission on Urban Life and Faith in early 2004, the National Secular Society said, 'Presumably (this report) will turn out to be just another propaganda exercise aimed at extracting further money from the public purse.'[14]

2.46   As Commissioners we are all too aware of the need to address public suspicion of religion and its motivations. Religious faith is by no means always a reasonable and liberal set of values which engender good citizenship and social cohesion. Government – and faith communities themselves – may need to recognize that religion has the potential to be divisive as well as cohesive.

2.47   There is also a danger that dwindling congregations in inner urban areas may be tempted to over-estimate the significance of their involvement in local projects, regardless of their actual impact.

2.48   Churches and other faith communities additionally need to beware of becoming 'co-opted' into government initiatives – delivering services that may compromise their independence. The Demos report, mentioned earlier, acknowledges, 'This resurgence of religious engagement with the wider community has coincided with the withdrawal of the state from direct provision of many services.' This poses a further question as to whether faith-based welfare should be deployed as an alternative to provision by the state, as it seems to have been in many parts of the United States. But the fact is, it offers a tangible and immediate means for faith communities to respond to the needs of their locality – a way of engaging directly with those most in need.

2.49   We challenge blanket references to 'faith' and 'faith communities' when thinking about their contribution to wider society. They are not necessarily as monochrome, docile and 'on-message' as statutory bodies might like. There needs to be a more nuanced and contextual understanding of how faith-based participation actually functions in specific circumstances.

Doing theology in the city

2.50   As we have already argued, theology – literally, 'talk about God' – is at the heart of the Commission. One of the tasks of the Commission has therefore been to flesh out a theological account of the nature of human community, and what it might mean to work for 'the good of the city'. So it is entirely appropriate that a major strand of the Commission's work focuses on values and visions – affirming the experiences and expectations of 'what makes a good city' as well as offering specific policy objectives. This is how we engage with the many 'delights, injustices and needs' of urban living in the light of the faithful capital.

2.51   But what can theology contribute? And how can it inform the choices and strategies of the urban Church? Chapter 3 of *Faith in the City* was devoted to a theological analysis of urban poverty. It was criticized for being influenced by 'liberation theology' which originated among the grassroots communities of

'Like potent secular ideologies, [religion] can unite or divide, include or exclude; it can provide the impetus to struggle for social justice or it can legitimize cruelty and oppression; it can promote social cohesion or conflict.'
Robert Furbey and Marie Macey, 'Religion and urban regeneration: a place for faith?' [13]

Latin America. Christianity, liberation theologians argue, is a *this-worldly* spirituality which regards social, economic and political transformation as an integral part of God's desire for the world.

2.52   In many respects, however, this part of *Faith in the City* was more an agenda for future development than a fully blown urban theology of liberation. Nevertheless, there are some aspects of its theology which sow the seeds for further development.

2.53   There was an emphasis on the need for the Church to publicly acknowledge the realities of social structures and economic systems as well as personal transformation. *Faith in the City* espoused a determination to move beyond simply ameliorating problems or delivering welfare work, to active engagement in their causes - challenging the public values underlying the shift to neo-liberalism.

Democratizing theology

2.54   *Faith in the City* emphasized the values of 'community', 'interdependence', 'mutuality' and 'solidarity'. These underpinned the principles of supporting disadvantaged individuals and communities, and required the Church to champion perspectives and ways of life that emerged from urban priority areas. In this respect, *Faith in the City* glimpsed an emergent theme of liberation theology that we now wish to make more explicit.

2.55   Theology is not just academics 'talking about God' - it is also 'the people's work'. We value the experiences of people who live in urban communities, who often experience the worst and most acute forms of poverty and social exclusion. This is not to romanticize their viewpoints, but to argue that the voices of resilience, service, grace and hope that have emerged from such situations deserve greater attention.

2.56   Reflecting on all this, we have developed three core themes which run through this report:

1] Theology is practical

2.57   People often regard theology as disconnected from the practice of everyday life and therefore irrelevant. Since *Faith in the City*, theologians have sought to overcome divisions between 'systematic' and 'applied' theology to talk about theology as primarily 'practical'.

2.58   This means two things.
- First, we understand theology as a resource for transformation. It enables people of faith to translate the inherited wisdom of their tradition into the practice of discipleship. So we see theology as the grammar of faithful practice - the discipline which offers a rich repository of stories, rules of life, values and visions by which people can faithfully live their lives under God.
- Secondly, we regard theology as 'performative'. It makes no sense to claim that theology is primarily or exclusively expressed in doctrinal statements or academic treatises. On the contrary, we understand that these propositions are derived from the incarnational principles already enacted and embodied in the liturgical, evangelistic, sacramental and practical/caring actions of faithful communities. The Church 'talks of God' fundamentally and quintessentially in its very activities of offering worship to God, in its life together and its outreach and care for others. In other words, theology takes place most authentically in the very practices of transformative faith-in-action (see box B2.1).

2] Everyday theologies

2.59   When *Faith in the City* declared that listening to the voices of local communities enabled the Commissioners to discover authentic 'faith in the city', we recognized that it was articulating a valuable truth. This was that it is not enough simply to develop a theology *for* the poor, but that we have to make space for the development of a theology *of* and *from* those experiencing poverty.

2.60   This is in keeping with a shift in academic theology from 'applied' theology to 'contextual' theology. This understands theological discourse as a 'performative' discipline, rooted in practical problems and reflecting its cultural setting as well as the insights of Christian tradition. *Faith in the City* also hinted at the possibility of giving voice to theologies which go beyond abstract, propositional statements of doctrine: a recognition that theological understandings are embodied in the narratives, liturgies, artistic expressions and corporate values of local congregations. [15]

2.61   In our enquiries, therefore, we have emphasized the stories, insights and experiences that emerge from urban communities of faith. We have tried to be attentive to what these understandings may have to say to the world at large. It is our way of genuinely exposing ourselves to 'the gospel of the poor' – of fostering voices 'from the underside' and encouraging the rest of the Church to acknowledge these voices as gifts to the wider Church.

2.62   We have therefore asked ourselves if there are ways in which urban theology can more accurately capture the concerns and cultures of urban communities – effectively, a 'theology of experience'.

2.63   We have called these 'everyday theologies', referring to the popular, the language of the streets, the vernacular, or what theologian Jeff Astley[17] terms 'ordinary theology'. We have tried to follow the work of theologians such as Robert Beckford and Anthony Reddie[18] who seek to merge liberation theology with 'black expressive cultures'. We are therefore looking for signs of new liturgies and expressions of spirituality and ways of exploring the person of Christ which speak more authentically from, and to, the lives of those in our urban areas.

3] Theology in public

2.64   We are also committed to conducting debate about the future of our cities *in public*. This means two things: first, it rejects any notion that religion is merely a private and personal matter. Rather, it should give shape and substance to our engagements with ethical, social and political matters – since theology is concerned with a God who is present and active in the whole of creation and the entirety of human concerns.

2.65   Secondly, this is a theology which should be prepared to actively engage in public debate. While theology provides the vocabulary of faithful action, it can never be simply the private language of a sectarian few, and it should be prepared to engage critically and constructively with alternative points of view.

'After ten years I thought our Church would be a Church *of* the poor and no longer talking as if it were a Church *for* the poor . . . is there a way of living, of worshipping, of acting, of operating, which will make the Church credible: not because of projects but because we are authentically living the faith of Jesus Christ in the communities where we are, in the way we worship, the way we pray, the way we act? I do not think we have shifted that much.'
Canon John Sentamu (now Archbishop of York) speaking to the Church of England General Synod [16]

It is clear that urban contexts are not spiritual deserts. Longing, hope, thanksgiving, celebration, penitence, lament, sorrow, forgiveness, healing and renewal are all evident [locally]. Through faithful Christian presence and some exemplary pastoral ministry, the Church has got a 'good name' again. Perhaps some of this energy and fortitude needs to become more explicit? Encouraging the churches to name what they dream of becoming and what they thank God and ask him for might be a constant source of spiritual development and a way of supporting each other on the journey.
Diocese of Newcastle, 2004

[B2.2

Life *and* **faith**

2.66　At the opening of the twenty-first century, the UK is a very different place from 1985. Yet cities continue to dominate our culture through the impact of their economic power and their sheer physical scale. But their influence reaches beyond the material and the visible - they occupy and stimulate our imaginations and inspire our dreams. For that reason, we argue that, substantial though the gains have been, strategies for the economic regeneration of our cities must not ignore the human, or spiritual dimension to visions of 'what makes a good city'.

2.67　For the urban churches, the legacy of *Faith in the City* has been a mixed blessing. It excites expectations, it creates opportunities, but it was also a product of its time. It cannot be repeated. The Church of England today sees more clearly that its establishment - with the echoes of past power and influence - sits uncomfortably with dwindling membership.

2.68　However, as far as the Government is concerned, religion (however sketchily that is perceived) still remains among the most significant elements of civil society and community mobilization. And, as a Commission, we have also heard time and again how shared service within local communities has given rise to opportunities for inter-faith dialogue and common purpose - and of the new opportunities these present for a united witness for the good of the city. These seem to us to focus around three themes:

- The renewed commitment to regeneration and neighbourhood renewal that is coming from many quarters;
- The intriguing use of language of human flourishing and spirituality in the hopes and visions for what makes a good city;
- The challenge to celebrate and support the many sources and expressions of faith which are taking place in the city.

2.69　British society - and urban England in particular - might be regarded as increasingly both 'post-Christian' and 'post-secular'.[19] Although there is undeniable numerical decline among the long-established churches, many other vibrant expressions of religion - including newer Christian expressions and the growth of other faiths - represent a significant and enduring public reality. Religious faith is still on the nation's agenda and is a vital part of the landscape of our cities and towns. Consequently, it is our view that this report offers compelling evidence that it is entirely appropriate to combine the twin ingredients of urban life and faith.

3 The World in Our Cities:
Diversity and Difference

3.1   'London: the world in one city', was the headline when the *Guardian* newspaper published a double-page map featuring a 'special celebration of the most cosmopolitan place on earth'.[1] The map identified 100 districts within the capital where high concentrations of people from different parts of the world live and work. Over 30% of London's residents in 2001 had been born outside England, more than 300 languages were spoken, and the city was home to at least 50 non-indigenous communities with populations of 10,000 or more.

3.2   The extraordinary cultural diversification of London is echoed in other cities across the country. As Leo Benedictus, who wrote the original Guardian article, added a year later, 'Altogether, between 1991 and 2001, the UK population increased by 2.2 million, some 1.14 million of whom were born abroad. And all this was before EU enlargement in May 2004, which pulled in 130,000 more people from the new member states in its first year alone.'[2] Many of the changes in urban life mentioned in the previous chapter can be seen either as advancing or reflecting this growing social 'diversity'. Our society was never as diverse as today, hosting people from scores of countries and every continent. This presents unprecedented opportunities and challenges – not just for government and society but also for the Church.

3.3   It is not difficult to pinpoint the two most pressing questions that this new situation throws up: 'Can we live together in our diversity?' and, if so, 'How?' We believe that we can and must live together and we argue that the emerging understanding of 'social capital' – in particular what we are calling 'faithful capital' – is central to enabling us to work out *how* to live together.

3.4   But no one should underestimate the difficulty of the task, because living with what is perceived as 'difference' challenges us all. We see the spectre of failure in political fanaticism, personal acts of racism and religious persecution, institutional practices of discrimination and, in particular, policies on political asylum in the United Kingdom. But our report also offers 'street-level' examples of how people of faith, as well as people of no religious commitment, are engaging positively with these issues.

What do we mean by 'diversity'?

3.5   The word 'diversity' here is shorthand for the differences between people that stem from their cultural experiences and attachments. Even our diversity is diverse! There is an understandable tendency to associate diversity with 'race' and ethnicity, but there is also variance in occupation, lifestyles, types of household, gender relations and youth cultures. There is sub-cultural diversity and fragmentation within music, sexuality, spirituality and religion, and politics. Almost nothing is monochrome. There are fewer fixed points and landmarks to help navigate an increasingly complex society. For many people, culture and personal identity are marked by fluidity, dispute, engagement and internal difference. Even those who pride themselves on being tolerant and inclusive – whether Christians or secular liberals – have difficulty in dealing with the resulting diversity and various understandings of a fully human and good life. In different ways, both are challenged by the growing cultural diversity of the United Kingdom.[4]

> 'Each one heard them speaking in the native language of each.'
> Acts 2.6

> 'O mankind! Behold, We have created you all from a male and female, and have made you nations and tribes, so that you might come to know one another.'
> Qur'an 49.13

> 'London in 2005 is uncharted territory. Never have so many different kinds of people tried living together in the same place before. What some people see as the greatest experiment of multiculturalism will triumph or fail here.'
> The *Guardian* [3]

3.6   Some issues (most obviously those of gender and sexuality) confront churches themselves with sharp challenges and are sources of deep conflict and division. These disputes affect the scope, conduct and effectiveness of urban ministry and the capacity to work with others. In this chapter, however, our main focus is on ethnic and religious *communal* diversity in English towns and cities.

3.7   At the outset, let us be clear that both faith and science agree that we are one human 'race'. Just as the Christian Scriptures find all people are made equal as image bearers of the divine, so biology finds that human beings form a single species, sharing common physical and mental structures and essential material and emotional needs.

'Every nation, tribe, language and people'

3.8   Of course, the intense diversity of London is not typical of England as a whole, still less the rest of the UK. Indeed, when asked, most people greatly overestimate the proportion of the population who are members of minority ethnic groups. In the 2001 Census, of a total UK population of nearly 58.8 million people, the total minority ethnic population was 4.6 million, that is, 7.9% of the total. Of these, 45% lived in London and a further 8% in the rest of the South East region. Elsewhere, 13% lived in the West Midlands, 8% in the North West, 8% in the East Midlands and 7% in Yorkshire and the Humber. By contrast, in the North East and the South West, the minority ethnic population constituted 2% of the total. With global migration patterns and political developments such as the expansion of the European community, this is changing all the time – often with quite unpredictable results.

3.9   The minority ethnic population in particular districts within the major urban conurbations of the North and the Midlands is often much greater than the regional average. And locally, there are important differences in the range and form of diversity. Outside London, Leicester is one of the more diverse cities with substantial Hindu, Muslim and Sikh communities. Bradford, on the other hand, has a proportionately very large minority ethnic population, but it is predominantly Pakistani Muslim. London's unique status as a truly diverse cosmopolis is clear.

3.10   Nevertheless, the experience of sharing neighbourhoods with people of different cultures and religious faiths is an increasingly common experience for people in many towns and cities. The 2001 Census included a question asking people to self-identify in terms of a religious faith. 77% did so. Of the 44 dioceses of the Church of England, 35 have parishes which are in some degree multi-faith. Within these latter dioceses 8.6% of the parishes have populations of which 10% or more of the residents are of other faiths. These predominantly urban parishes accounted for 23% of the English population.[5]

       Diversity is not new. Kenneth Leech, an Anglican priest and acknowledged commentator on urban affairs, observes that 'most white British people do not seem to realize that immigration to Britain has been an integral part of its history for centuries'. In addition to the European Celtic, Roman, Saxon, Norman and Dutch Protestant legacies, 'black people too have been residents of the country for a very long time, probably going back to the Roman invasion'.[6] Migration is integral to the history of humanity as people experience hardship or sense opportunity.

3.12   But we are living at a time when the 'pushes' and 'pulls' that prompt migration are especially intense. Present conditions of global inequality, commercial expansion, environmental degradation, oppression, war and famine, together with new opportunities for mobility and communication, all encourage uniquely large 'flows' of people.

3.13   Globalization, with its reduction of the constraints of geography and its web of instant communication, may initially seem to suggest the remorseless invasion and increasing homogeneity of localities stemming from the economic and cultural power of trans-national corporations, financial markets and world media. Yet it has become increasingly clear that globalization has not eradicated local cultural diversity. In Edward Soja's oft-quoted epithet, if 'everywhere the local is becoming globalized', it is simultaneously the case that 'the global is becoming localized'.[7] In cities around the world people encounter the opportunities and challenges of living in distinctive places marked increasingly by many forms of diversity.

No easy path

3.14   'Diversity' is an overworked term, often invoked in naïvely optimistic expressions of an urban 'melting pot' where everyone enjoys increasing (and disposable) lifestyle and identity options in an expanding cultural market. Missing from this picture is the often brutally tangible experience of racism and its associated fear and exclusion. The response to local diversity and perceived 'difference' is often a combination of defensive retreat and active aggression, rather than welcoming acceptance and engagement.

3.15   Of course, fear of the poor and the 'strange' newcomer – reflected in residential segregation – is a dominant theme in English urban history. What is different today is the perceived threat of globalization. This brings with it the uncertainties of mobile capital, flexible labour markets, declining governmental legitimacy, the erosion of collective welfare and the transfer of risk to individuals.[8] The search for security and certainty in a world of fewer fixed points is greatly intensified. This response is graphically expressed by Zygmunt Bauman:

> And what are the abandoned, de-socialized and atomized lonely individuals likely to dream of, and given a chance, do? Once the big harbours have been closed or stripped of the breakwaters that used to make them secure, the hapless sailors will be inclined to carve out and fence off their own small havens where they can anchor and deposit their bereaved, and fragile, identities. No longer trusting the public navigation network, they will jealously guard access to such private havens against all and any intruders.'[10]

3.16   This 'jealous guarding' of 'private havens' against 'intruders' signals the potential of fear, turning to aggression and a battle for 'territory', both physical and metaphorical. Consequently, there is a new significance of 'the local' in a globalizing world – including local politics and local collective actions. But, as Bauman adds, what underlies the search for security by urban dwellers is disorientation, fear, anxiety and aggression. And its manifestations are found everywhere, from the very affluent in their 'gated communities', to marginalized poor people in decaying neighbourhoods, to the turf wars of gangs of young people.

3.17   The deep-seated need for belonging and identity easily breeds a suspicion of the 'other'. The more obvious the difference and the more easily identifiable the 'other' is, the easier it is for antipathy to grow.

3.18   The major denominations are confronted by diversity, both within their established congregations and by new congregations drawn from a multiplicity of global cultures. There are important lessons from this experience that must be learned and shared in order to help both ourselves as people of faith and others to traverse this uncharted territory.

Humanity on the move

People have always been on the move and they have moved great distances. There are many impulses behind these movements: victorious armies and empires have swept across and implanted themselves into new territories; the defeated and dispossessed have fled to a defensible land and safer havens; the enslaved have been torn from their homes and relocated in the lands of the enslaver; the underemployed and unemployed have searched for work; the persecuted have sought asylum; the curious and adventurous have always been travelling, drifting and exploring. [9]

[B3.1]

Young people: diversity and common culture

While research finds significant prejudice based on skin colour in contemporary western society, one area where there is evidence of a common culture across racial divides is that forged by the music of urban life. Lyrics which speak of the trials and tribulations of urban living as well as the hope, signify the power of music to engage and connect young people, regardless of their ethnic origin.

The rise of the Music Television Network (MTV)[11] has tapped into the aspirations and world of a global teenage audience. Simultaneously, the rise of hip-hop from New York's Bronx has led to unique British expressions of this distinctive urban music. The MoBo (Music of Black Origin) Awards[12] reflect this growth, including a vital new genre in the UK called 'Urban Gospel'.[13]

Rap has become a major contender in the global market of teen's culture. In the past 30 years, hip-hop has gone from Ghetto streets to the corporate suites, selling everything from music and clothes to brand names . . . hip-hop has now become mainstream for the entire planet.

Current studies indicate that major companies trying to advertise to the total youth-to-young adult population look to trends in the urban community. So many suburban kids shed their preppy look to embrace urban cool; you see it in clothes, the musical styles, the dance, language and so forth. Rap music's no. 1 consumer has been the white suburban male purchasing 65% to 70% of the art form consecutively for the past 8 years. Because of its strong emotional qualities and it's ability to convey thought directly and innovatively hip-hop has become radical poetry of post-modernism; ranging from kids on street corners to school lunch rooms to Hip Hop Operas like MTV's award winning production Carmen Brown the modern take from the classical opera Carmen.

Fred Lynch [14]   [B3.2]

Street level antipathy and racism

3.19   Antipathy and prejudice based on skin colour remains widespread and shows little sign of diminishing, even in the context of growing ethnic diversity. Research requested for the Commission indicated that 35% of young people living in cities and 31% (41% in the case of males) of those living in large towns felt that the movement of people of different ethnic groups in Britain should be restricted.[15] Furthermore, almost a quarter of young white men believe that there are too many black people in the country, a proportion that rises still further among respondents in the south of England. These findings are consistent with those of research funded by the Joseph Rowntree Foundation published in 2005.[16] We cannot assume, therefore, that by itself familiarity or daily association with people of different colour and ethnicity brings, greater acceptance.

3.20   But other evidence points in a gloomier direction. Racist incidents recorded by the police in 2003/04 rose by 7% to 52,694. In the same year there were 35,022 racially or religiously aggravated offences recorded by the police.[17] Over half of these were instances of harassment. The actual number of incidents and offences are certainly much higher as many go unreported. The British Crime Survey suggests that between 130,000 and 140,000 racist incidents occur each year.

3.21   The reference to 'religiously aggravated offences' raises the growing issue of discrimination and persecution on grounds of religious faith. The Home Office combines the 'ethnic' and 'religious' categories, which reflects the difficulty in identifying the motivation of attacks and making a clear distinction. Nevertheless, recent years have brought growing concerns regarding harassment and attacks directed at people on grounds of religion prompting controversial proposals for legislation. There is no doubt that there has been a rise in attacks and harassment against Jews and Muslims.[18]

3.22   The events of 9/11 in the USA and of 7 and 21 July 2005 in London have underlined the development of 'Islamophobia', a term given initial currency by the Runnymede Trust in 1997.[19] Hostility to Muslims has increased in Britain and other European countries – the European Union Monitoring Centre (EUMC) on racism and xenophobia identified a significant rise in physical and verbal attacks on Muslims and a heightened climate of discrimination after 9/11.[20] 'Islamophobia' targets Muslims, not because of skin colour or cultural background or land of origin but because of religious affiliation. We should not forget that people from a wider range of religious faiths and traditions, such as Hindus and Sikhs, are also affected.

3.23   The continuing prevalence of ethnic and religious discrimination by individuals and groups at 'street level' works against attempts to secure equality, freedom, understanding, trust and confidence on which a flourishing, socially diverse society can be built. These problems gain momentum when fear and lack of knowledge among many are co-ordinated by extremists.

Organized antipathy and racism

3.24   The xenophobic movements of twentieth-century Europe harnessed uncertainty and fear which stemmed from economic insecurity and deprivation and a loss of confidence in government. For all the changes of the last two generations, similar experiences have produced a disturbingly familiar dynamic in particular in English urban localities. This has been most notable in some former English textile towns and, in the early 1990s, the Isle of Dogs, East London.

3.25   Although the British National Party (BNP) is much smaller and less influential than parallel organizations in western Europe, at particular moments it has provided an interpretation of urban problems that feeds on resentment of 'the stranger', exploits grievances and offers a misguided sense of purpose. It is a purpose that flatly rejects the vision of a hard-won and celebrated diversity. The aim of the BNP is:

> to secure a future for the indigenous peoples of these islands in the North Atlantic which have been our homeland for millennia. We use the term indigenous to describe the people whose ancestors were the earliest settlers here after the last great Ice Age and which have been complemented by the historic migrations from mainland Europe.[21]

3.26   There is no reference here to 'securing a future' for people with family histories in other parts of the world or of other ethnicities or non-white skin colour. Indeed, the BNP is committed to 'a system of voluntary resettlement' of people who it deems to have family origins outside Europe, an immediate halt to all immigration, and a 'clamp down' on what it terms the 'flood' of asylum seekers. For many British citizens and people seeking refugee status, the aim is to create insecurity and fear. The agenda is exclusion based on a mistaken view that people who are not white do not belong to the human race.

3.27   The BNP has significant influence in articulating anxiety, fear and hatred and in encouraging the stereotyping, harassment and violence that denies the very legitimacy of the question, 'How can we live together?' While it remains marginal in electoral terms, it punches above its weight. Its main impact is arguably through its influence on mainstream political parties and the parameters of national debate on multiculturalism and immigration. It helps to sustain an undercurrent of xenophobia which is not countered, but accommodated, in legislation and in institutional policy and practices.

Institutional racism and discrimination

3.28   For over two decades research has pointed to the importance of institutional as well as personal racism and discrimination. The term 'institutional racism' came into popular recognition after the Stephen Lawrence Inquiry's criticisms of the Metropolitan Police. It refers to the way in which, consciously or unconsciously, organizational structures and procedures are developed which disadvantage, oppress and discriminate against particular people and groups.

3.29   In addition to the institutional policies and practices of public organizations, private sector employers and other commercial organizations, the immigration legislation of successive Governments has been a key 'institutional' source of inequality and social division. Peter Dwyer is one of many commentators who have seen much immigration legislation as helping 'to define the presence of black people in Britain as problematic', expressing a 'racialized notion of "Britishness"', and embodying the view that 'difference is a "problem"'.[22]

3.30   For many people of minority ethnic origin, there is a gulf between their formal status as citizens and their actual life experiences. Reviewing the evidence in 2000, the UK Government's Social Exclusion Unit found that:

> In comparison to their representation in the population, people from minority ethnic communities are more likely than others to live in

deprived areas; be poor; be unemployed, compared to white people with similar qualifications; suffer ill health and live in crowded unpopular housing. They also experience widespread racial harassment and racial crime and are over-represented in the criminal justice system . . . but there is much variation within and between groups in all of these areas.[23]

3.31   Policy has often been formulated in rapid response to popular xenophobia at particular moments of tension, sustained by a large section of the press on a political terrain influenced by fanaticism. If we understand 'difference' as an opportunity for mutual enrichment, then policies on political asylum in the UK of successive Governments, Conservative and Labour, pose a particular obstacle.

3.32   A host of confusions and myths surround refugees, asylum seekers,[24] illegal immigrants and economic migrants. These are assiduously cultivated by sections of the press, helping to make asylum the third most important issue for the British public in 2003. They include claims that Britain is a 'soft touch' for asylum seekers and refugees; that asylum seekers come looking for – and receive – generous welfare benefits; that they 'jump the queue' for housing and health services, that they are a criminal threat, and that they are unskilled and will act as a drain on the British economy.

3.33   These assertions are countered by the Refugee Council.[25] Meanwhile, government constraints on welfare entitlements for asylum seekers, the complexity of the varying statuses of applications, and inefficiencies in administration, are producing extreme poverty, even destitution. Many have to rely on non-statutory bodies, including refugee agencies, refugee community organizations, charities, churches and other faith organizations and family and friends.

3.34   We believe that the historic communities of faith have a critical role to play in contributing to the healing of a society fractured in its response to diversity. But before exploring the ways in which religion can celebrate diversity and promote social cohesion, we are bound to note that religion too has played a part in fuelling tension.

When religion is part of the problem

3.35   Religion exists in the same context of anxiety and uncertainty as everything else. So the contribution of faith to how people can live good lives together in diversity must be a subject of honest reflection by people of all faiths. All the major faith traditions have beliefs and ethics that inspire community service, co-operation, peacemaking, the pursuit of social justice, and the acceptance of others. However, we have also witnessed the growth of what has been called 'furious religion',[26] provoked by the exposure of religious traditions to secularism and to other religions. Malise Ruthven identifies the growth of 'a "religious way of being" that manifests itself in a strategy by which beleaguered believers attempt to preserve their distinctive identity as a people or group in the face of modernity and secularization'.[27]

3.36   This religious retreat into certainty can be read as a particular expression of the wider cultural uncertainty and anxiety and the search for a 'safe haven'. Its capacity for creating destructive division and conflict is clear. Elsewhere in this report we provide strong evidence for the major and effective Christian commitment to building trust between different people and groups. However, we are forced also to confront the darker aspect of religion. As the Bishop of Oxford, Richard Harries, admits:

There is a particular danger in religion . . . For all religions claim to mediate the absolute. It is easy to topple over the brink and identify that absolute with the finite and fallible human structures through which that absolute is disclosed to human beings. In short, religion can

Asylum and destitution

'My experience comes from my involvement with a destitution project that provides food and, if possible, shelter. The first person we housed was made destitute at the time of her claim because it was felt she hadn't claimed asylum soon enough after arriving in the UK. It was alleged that she had waited two days and was therefore fraudulent. (Her lawyer had made a mistake in processing her claim.) The other person had lost his claim for asylum but there was no safe route for him to return home. We personally as a family have done very little compared to others in the city who regularly house complete strangers because of this situation. In Manchester about 500–600 folk are destitute, about 200 in Sheffield and 350 in Wales (figures from Boaz Trust and ASSIST).'

Revd Sarah Schofield, St Philip's, Gorton, Manchester

reinforce religious communities and religious organizations in being impervious to criticism and thinking their claims override all others, even basic human rights. [28]

3.37 Equally damaging is when people of faith simply fail to challenge the forces which attack diversity. The major Christian denominations in England, would certainly assent to the Church of England's 2004 Commission on Racial Justice statement:

An individual has value because God values him or her as equal in dignity and human worth. We are human beings together, and as Christians we are called to love one another as Christ loves us . . . Before God there is only one race: the human race, created in God's own image, and loved as God's children and friends.'[29]

3.38 Nevertheless, Christians have not always lived out these principles. As the European historian Kenneth Medhurst has observed, the record of churches in fighting against Fascism during the inter-war years was poor,[30] reminding us that neither Protestant nor Catholic Christian history, is undefiled by racism. For example, while Jewish people have been a part of English 'diversity' for many centuries, the practice of Christian churches and people in accepting and respecting Jewish people (both religious and secular) has often been, at best, grudging and, at worst, shocking. Today, many local churches still do not identify a commitment to the politics of racial justice as central to their faith and mission. All this warns us that the 'celebration of diversity' cannot be allowed to stand as a cheap lifestyle slogan. There is no easy path to a good and diverse life together.

Can faith be part of the solution?

3.39 As part of the Commission's investigation into 'What makes a Good City?' people in Plymouth organized a multi-faith event, attracting over 200 people. The aim was to alert more people to the day-to-day hardships experienced by asylum seekers in their city.

3.40 The stress on personal stories proved to be both powerful, and, for some participants, shocking. Many were completely unaware that such traumatic events were happening in Plymouth. People heard that there were immediate needs, ranging from financial donations to the provision of supplies such as sleeping bags, food, toiletry and hygiene items. Volunteer help was needed for transport, administration and for helping asylum seekers to put together their basic information prior to their first interviews with representatives of the Home Office.

3.41 Out of this came not only pledges of assistance from 40 people but 70 people came to a follow-up meeting and plans began to be drawn up for short-term accommodation, friendship schemes and more. One refugee said of the occasion, 'I have never felt so supported and honoured in Plymouth. Thank you.'

3.42 At the heart of this example lies a practical principle which is distinctive to people of faith. This is the imperative to move beyond mere 'tolerance' of diversity. 'Tolerance' is one of the watchwords of a liberal society, but it is essentially passive. Christians and adherents of many other faiths would understand that the proper response to the stranger is more proactive – it is expressed in the biblical practice of 'hospitality'.

3.43 Tolerance is the response of the powerful to the less powerful. It carries no imperative to actively help those who are vulnerable, whereas hospitality calls us to enter into relationship with those who are different. Hospitality is a central biblical theme, particularly evident in the teachings of Jesus and his answer to the question 'Who is my neighbour?'. The Christian tradition defines our neighbour as 'the stranger', someone who lacks the resources to sustain a 'place' in society. Hospitality certainly means 'entertaining strangers', but it can require a changing of one's own life and understanding in the process (Hebrews 13.2). This is precisely what happened in Plymouth.

Commitment to hospitality

The Christian commitment to hospitality is reflected in this extract from a recent challenge to government:

Statement for the end of the destitution of asylum seekers
We believe that it is inhuman and unacceptable that some asylum seekers are left homeless and destitute by Government policies. Every city has people destitute or living on food parcels because they have no means of support. We support Church Action on Poverty's call to change the policies that make refused asylum seekers destitute. As a society we have international moral and legal responsibilities to welcome those fleeing from adversity in other parts of the world and provide social security. But the threat of destitution is being used as a way of pressuring refused asylum seekers to leave the country. There are many asylum seekers who have their cases refused but have no safe route to return or whose travel documents cause logistical problems for removal. There are also many cases where people are unjustly refused asylum.

Church Action on Poverty [31]

[B3.3

3.44   Similarly, in South London, South London Citizens, a coalition of faith and secular organizations who campaign on key community issues, undertook a 'listening' exercise. A member of a church congregation described her experience of poor administration, poor facilities and lack of human dignity at Lunar House in Croydon (where the UK's asylum and immigration claims are handled). Out of this arose an enquiry into the workings at Lunar House (see box B3.4).

Faithful campaigning in South London   [B3.4

During a 'consultative forum' organized by South London Citizens, a coalition of faith and secular organizations who campaign on key community issues, a church member described her experience of poor administration, poor facilities and lack of human dignity at Lunar House in Croydon, the centre where UK asylum and immigration claims are handled. Hers was not an isolated tale; many others told similar stories. Significantly, two workplace representatives of the Public and Commercial Services Union, which represents the workforce at Lunar House and the Home Office, heard the woman's testimony. One of the PCS representatives apologized on behalf of the workforce at Lunar House, and explained the pressures staff were under. It was to be the beginnings of the Lunar House Enquiry.

In order to highlight concerns at Lunar House, a group of 'commissioners' were appointed to oversee the Enquiry and three 'actions' held. First, a day of public hearings was convened with Commissioner where non-governmental and voluntary organizations provided testimonies on the asylum and immigration process at Lunar House. Academics lamented the queues and cost of extending student visas, a Zimbabwean woman under *the care of the Gatwick Detainees Welfare Group told of how officials treated her with disrespect and aggression, while a Rwandan girl of 17, the victim of rape and trafficking, described explaining the circumstances of her application in a public room where others could hear everything. Other groups who contributed included the Albanian Community, Asylum Aid, the Jesuit Refugee Group, Balham, Battersea and East London Mosques and the Immigration and Asylum Service.*

Secondly, survey forms were circulated to staff and users at Lunar House and volunteers worked over three days, helped by the priest and congregation at St Dominic's Parish, Waddon. Finally, a public hearing at the House of Lords focused on the Immigration and Nationality Directorate, and representatives responded to the concerns put to them by the Commissioners.

This 'bottom-up' process contrasts starkly with media and party political discourse on asylum and immigration. The faith groups and trade unions of the South London Citizens demonstrate not only that people are concerned at the treatment of migrants arriving in the UK, but that they will put in time and energy in order to humanize the operation of our migration system.

The call to actively welcome the poor and excluded which is embodied in the teachings of the major religions is eloquent testimony to the notion of faithful capital explored in Chapter 1 of this report. It is something articulated particularly clearly in the Rule and tradition of the Benedictine monastic order. (see box 3.5).

Hospitality is a positive celebration of diversity. Instead of treating the 'other' as a threat to be barricaded against, we should be opening ourselves to the experience, turning strangers into friends, welcoming the cooking, the conversation and the culture they bring to the party. [32]

3.45   Hospitality is an important aspect of faithful capital. It is about the centrality of 'relationship' to human flourishing. In this way faithful capital is located as an aspect of social capital, the value of which is in human relationships and social networks. A distinction is commonly made between three types of social capital – 'bonding', 'bridging' and 'linking' – which provides a more penetrating understanding of the qualities of social networks and which is particularly helpful in relation to hospitality in the context of diversity. These types are elaborated by Alison Gilchrist:

- Bonding – based on enduring, multi-faceted relationships between similar people with strong mutual commitments such as among friends, family and other close-knit groups.
- Bridging – formed from the connections between people who have less in common, but may have overlapping interests; for example, between neighbours, colleagues, or between different groups within a community.
- Linking – derived from the links between people or organizations beyond peer boundaries, cutting across status and similarity and enabling people to exert influence and reach resources outside their normal circles.[33]

3.46   Of course, these types are never quite as clear-cut as they appear. For example, through making bridges and links with people who we see as 'different' from ourselves, we may over time develop the degree of trust that produces 'bonds' between us. Also, the sense of acceptance, love and self-worth that stems from good bonding, especially in our younger years, often provides us with the confidence to engage in the challenges of bridging and linking.

3.47   The experience of church life is a good example of this. It would be easy to assume that members of a church congregation are similar, 'bonded', people. But this is rarely the case. Congregations are often diverse and make significant demands on an individual's ability to 'bridge' with people who, through age, gender, marital status, sexuality, ethnicity, language, occupation and past life experiences have developed their particular character. However, congregations are sometimes unable to live with this diversity, resulting in a microcosm of the tensions and xenophobia experienced in the world beyond the church's doors. Difference places strong demands on the quality of leadership and – if a congregation is to grow – it will need to learn its own lessons of hospitality and develop the skills and qualities of conciliation.

3.48   Good churches are places where people are nurtured through bonding and early experiences of participation that equip them for the challenges of developing bridging and linking social capital, first within their 'home' congregation, and then with others in the wider community who have shared objectives. We should not underestimate the role of churches as contexts in which social networkers, who later move to a wider stage, can develop.

3.49   What took place in the Isle of Dogs in 1993 is a good example of what can happen when bridges are made across faith and community (see box B3.6).

3.50   Christians and their communities, along with people of other faiths and none, make an enormous contribution as they work with others to develop relationships which extend beyond bonding to the development of the bridges and links which are crucial to the well-connected community and the good city. This work is already taking place, but there is still much to do and this requires openness to mutual learning. Christians have a great deal to learn from secular

St Benedict and hospitality

Hospitality is one of the key components of the Benedictine lifestyle. There is no Benedictine spirituality without the welcoming of guests. In his Rule, Saint Benedict, who lived in the sixth century, says 'Let all guests that come to the monastery be received as Christ. For, one day, he will say: "I was a stranger and you welcomed me".' In other words, monastic hospitality is essentially based on Christian values. As one recent Benedictine writer put it, 'When we accept, we take an open stance to the other person. It is more than merely piously tolerating them. We stand in the same space and we appreciate who they are, right now at this moment, and affirm the Sacred in them. And in this way, we too are changed. This is the essence of hospitality.'

[B3.5

Prayer and action for a multi-ethnic Britain

Sometimes the Church has a particularly strategic role to play in nurturing diversity in contemporary urban settings. One example comes from the Isle of Dogs in London. The area had been the focus of a globally driven restructuring of property, employment, land use, and population change. A rawness was felt by the local working-class population which felt squeezed out of their locality by forces beyond their control. The equally marginalized Asian population found they were often the victims of a growing resentment. This came to a sharp focus, in September 1993, when a BNP candidate, Derek Beackon, was elected as the party's first local government councillor. By the following May, despite winning a higher number of votes, he was out of office. Kenneth Leech and Nicholas Holtam were local clergy at the time. Fr Leech takes up the story:

'The defeat of Beackon was the result of an alliance between the Christian churches, the Samuda Women's Centre, the Bengali Action Group and the trades unions. The role of the churches was extremely important. From the moment that Beackon was elected, it was decided that a community worker would be employed with the express object of undermining the roots of the fascist vote. Through the help of the Joseph Rowntree Charitable Trust a community worker, Sue Mayo, was appointed, and her role in the defeat of the BNP was of critical importance. It was a major example of a local parish acting in an analytic and prophetic way.'[34]

The importance of good information was recognized in commissioning research on the social and economic character of the area and, in the shadow of the 'regeneration' of the London Docklands Development Corporation, funds were secured for 'voter education' and monitoring opinion. Detailed 'slog' was undertaken in getting people registered to vote but it was also understood that intellectual argument and organization were not enough unless the feelings and emotions of disaffected and disillusioned people in this part of London were to be respectfully addressed. Nicholas Holtam describes the installation of two graffiti boards in the church marked, 'How do you feel?' and the other 'What can we do?' The responses were shared with ministers and church members at other churches as a basis for prayer and action and to work out an agenda. In this way, fatalism was addressed and people were energized by participation. In the neighbourhood, 'local residents were asked to make positive statements and to make it visible that they were in favour of a multi-cultural society . . . In the end more than one mile of rainbow ribbon was cut into small strips and looped. Wearing this ribbon indicated your support for a multicultural Isle of Dogs. It changed the atmosphere of fatalism to one where the majority of people were in favour of "a rainbow people".'[35]

The campaign involved emotion, intellect and observation and churches worked closely with a wide range of other community and faith groups grasping the 'local culture of urgency'. It was only one battle at a particular moment and as the wider issues of housing, employment, education and community relations remain a matter of continuing contest and debate. It was a costly endeavour – people involved were regularly threatened, but it was important in building trust and mutual respect with people outside the churches and significant development within churches. The long-term presence of churches helps in keeping memories and provides a basis for a continuing response to local needs and the pursuit of justice.

partners and people of other faiths who share a vision of a just and peaceful plural society.[36] By definition, bridging and linking faithful capital must stem from a respect born of careful listening and the affirmation of the goodwill and achievements of others.

3.51   In Leicester we have witnessed the contribution of faith to the development of strong bridging and linking faithful capital in this diverse city. Here we see a particular example of a more universal application revealed in the recent research funded by the Joseph Rowntree Foundation.[37] This identifies the resources that people of faith, including Christians, can offer when they work with others and draw on their own distinctive resources.

3.52   There are dangers in using a single example. What happens in Leicester cannot be regarded as a blueprint for application in another city. There are economic, leadership and faith factors, all of which are peculiar to this city. Nevertheless, the Leicester story does exemplify what we as a Commission have also found to be taking place in countless instances elsewhere.

3.53   There are at least four ways in which we see this taking place. First we see evidence in Leicester of the importance of the bridges provided by the strong and growing inter-faith and faith-secular networks, and the mutual understanding and trust which the associational 'spaces' of faith can bring. These seem to have been significant in permitting co-ordinated and agreed responses to the challenges of diversity. Bonding has also developed between people of different faiths and of no religious faith as they have worked together over an extended period.

3.54   Secondly, in line with the Rowntree findings, we see here a particular example of the wider strong engagement by faiths in formal local governance.

3.55   Thirdly, in the large number of 'faith' social projects in Leicester we see evidence of the motivation and empowerment for civil involvement that can stem from faithful belief, practice and participation.

3.56   Fourthly, the faith buildings and premises which provide the venues for the majority of these projects underline a national pattern. The physical capital resources of faith organizations are used increasingly to generate faithful capital, especially when the 'host' worshipping community is willing to take risks and relinquish some control.

3.57   Christians and people of other faiths can clearly bring distinctive 'gifts'. But we also see signs of some of the barriers and tensions that surround faithful capital. There are two particular issues.

3.58   First, there are inequalities between faiths in their capacity to engage and to develop faithful capital in the city. The prominence of the Church of England in particular, but closely followed by the other major Christian denominations, retains the capacity to lead in forging links with government and in facilitating the development of bridging networks (this is a national pattern and not peculiar to Leicester). Anglicans are still relatively rich in terms of personnel, premises, training and other resources. While other faiths often welcome the access that the established Church can give them to government and governance, there is, nevertheless an issue of power here which needs to be recognized and addressed.

3.59   Secondly, as we mentioned earlier, faith congregations and organizations can be places of oppression and marginalization for particular members. The Rowntree research identified the status of women and young people as particularly significant. For them the 'spaces' of faith can be restricting or oppressive. But there is evidence that several of these obstacles have been recognized in the joint report produced by the Diocese of Leicester, the Leicester Council of Faiths and Voluntary Action Leicester. This was particularly clear in the importance placed on co-ordinating and sharing resources, and in identifying the importance of extending faith participation in a young people's council of faith. We need to work with young people and we commend the work of the Intercultural and Communication Leadership School (ICLS) in Leicester.

Leicester – bridges, links and cohesion

In 2003 the City of Leicester was awarded beacon status for community cohesion. It is not a non-racist or non-discriminatory paradise but it is widely seen as both ethnically and religiously diverse and socially cohesive.

Leicester is extremely diverse. Hindus, Muslims and Sikhs are all seen as major stakeholders in the city, possibly helping to dissipate tensions that may occur between two single communities. Highly complex interactions occur between these groups, often stemming from religious affinity. Even outside religious association, there is also the impact of inter-marriage, cross-cultural influence and inter-ethnic competition (especially in the economic and educational realms) – all of which make it difficult to isolate one group to study it or contrast it with others. It may be that this complexity among the minority communities of Leicester is actually part of the explanation for Leicester's positive reputation.

While policy makers, politicians and community leaders in Leicester are all keen to assert that there must be no complacency, they nevertheless identify in the city an atmosphere in which a basic level of trust exists between leaders of different communities. Also the mechanism and relationships are present to deal with tensions as and when they arise. The visible celebration of diversity and the pro-active migration policies of the City Council have created a space where ethnic minorities feel comfortable – they are not under any pressure to assimilate to a single cultural norm. There is significant social bridging and linking as well as bonding evident among many minority ethnic households.

But also of clear significance is the faithful capital of Christian churches and other faiths. The leadership within the Diocese of Leicester has been very important in this respect. Successive bishops have seen it as their role to mediate between members of other faith groups where tensions have occurred or potential conflicts have arisen; for example after 9/11 and 7/7, during the Hindu-Muslim conflict in Gujarat, or in the context of tensions in the Middle East. The Faith Leaders Forum, a body working in addition to the Leicester Council of Faiths, was convened after 9/11 and has adopted the principle of 'an attack on one is an attack on all' in rallying behind the Muslim community when the threat to people and properties was suspected. The bonds between faith leaders and people, the bridges between faiths and the links with national and local government have been important in sustaining cohesion and in celebrating diversity.

There is a broad base of social action among the faith organizations of Leicester. A study of the Diocese of Leicester, the Leicester Council of Faiths, and Voluntary Action Leicester identified 250 faith groups operating nearly 450 projects.[38]This report looked to the future, recommending a series of exchange visits between faith groups; support for a faith regeneration network; the mutual training and resourcing of faith communities to engage and deliver more effectively with the well-being of the local communities; and the formation of a young people's council of faith.

3.60   One of the most contentious areas of overlap between communities of faith in a diverse society is in education, particularly in relation to faith schools. This is not just an issue of contention between believers and non-believers, but among believers themselves. Many Christians, for example, choose to exercise their faith in a commitment to schools with no special faith ethos. All people of faith desire good educational opportunities for all children. Nonetheless, more than a quarter of state primary schools and almost 6% of state secondary schools are Church of England institutions. A further 100 new Church of England secondary schools are in the pipeline, while some 10% of children in primary and secondary education in the state sector attend Roman Catholic schools.

3.61   As cities become more diverse, one risk is that different ethnic, racial or religious groups co exist in parallel communities which have few points of contact or common ground. A growing body of influential opinion argues that faith schools exacerbate this situation. So while the issue of such schools is not specific to cities, it is peculiarly significant to urban areas because of the importance of social cohesion in the face of high levels of diversity.

3.62   But pointing a finger at faith-based schools for fostering antipathy between ethnic groups all too often diverts attention from a more fundamental threat to social cohesion – that of 'white flight' out of neighbourhoods that become ethnically mixed. The inclination of white households and professionals to quit ethnically diverse areas of our cities – often to seek wider educational opportunities – fundamentally undermines social cohesion.

3.63   The Commission recognizes the misgivings of some, and would share some of that concern if a particular school becomes sectarian or elitist. But we assert that faith schools should be understood as having a 'foundation in a faith' and not as 'schools for the faithful'. Such faithful foundations are widely respected and sought after by parents, not least because they help provide a rounded, 'holistic' and distinctive values-based approach to education which has real merit.

3.64   But we recognize that faith schools have more work to do in opening-up selection procedures. Eligibility for a school place needs to be based on a demonstrable willingness to support the school's *ethos* rather than belonging to a particular denomination or faith. We want to see faith schools (of all kinds) be more open and inclusive than they are. We commend those many schools where this approach is already evident and where, for instance, children from families of church adherents are outnumbered by those from other religious faiths or none.

3.65   We also contend that respect for different faith traditions in a diverse society is greatly enhanced by having an understanding of faiths other than one's own. All schools need to encourage students to take seriously the relevance of the resources of faith and which aim to promote awareness and confidence in relation to faiths other than the student's own.

3.66   A significant theme running throughout this report argues that personal well-being and 'pro-social' behaviour is strongly linked to having a sense of purpose in life, which in turn is closely associated – although not exclusively – with religious faith. Given the decline of involvement in formal (Christian) religion, faith schools have an important role in giving confidence to the exploration of intuitions and concerns in relation to faith. Giving respect to others and being attentive to their needs have deep – if not exclusive – roots in 'faithful capital' and these values are vital in making a good city which celebrates diversity.

3.67   The ability to celebrate and live with 'difference' as a source of human enrichment is a key urban challenge. We draw strength from what is taking place in Leicester and affirm that where active welcome and hospitality can supercede the passive qualities of tolerance, then a genuine celebration of diversity can take place. By making neighbours out of strangers we remove the spectres of fear and animosity that have dogged urban areas for centuries.

Breaking down the barriers

The Inter Cultural Leadership School (ICLS) runs a programme in Leicester once a year and invites 'pre-influential' or prospective leaders from diverse faith groups and ethnic backgrounds to a residential training programme in leadership and conflict resolution. The participants are between eighteen and thirty. There is a strong focus on pre-conceived stereotypes and perceptions and how to break down the barriers between different cultures and religions which make up a community. Each course produces active members of the ICLS 'Network of Trust' who build on their experiences by making presentations to other organizations and developing projects towards furthering community understanding.

[B3.8

4 Prosperity:

In Pursuit of Well-being

4.1   Our society faces two major paradoxes of prosperity. First, most of us have become more prosperous in the past 20 years, yet the gap between the rich and poor has widened. As a society we are more unequal than ever. [1] Despite the introduction of the minimum wage, and the lowest rate of unemployment for around 30 years, some people still go hungry while the already wealthy can net bonuses worth millions.

4.2   Secondly, there is no evidence that even those who have benefited most from the new prosperity are greatly happier. Much evidence suggests they are short on life satisfaction – they experience unease over crime, personal relationships, mental health and basic trust of others.

4.3   If we are to achieve well-being in Britain, we need to resolve both of these paradoxes.

4.4   In this chapter, we explore what is behind this situation. Since *Faith in the City*, several church reports have addressed questions of economic justice. These include:

- The Roman Catholic reports, *The Common Good* (English and Welsh Bishops, 1996), and *Prosperity with a Purpose* (Irish Bishops);
- The Salvation Army's report *The Paradox of Prosperity* (1999);
- The ecumenical reports *Unemployment and the Future of Work* (CTBI 1997)and, more recently, *Prosperity with a Purpose - Christians and the Ethics of Affluence* (CTBI, 2005).

4.5   The work of Christian non-governmental organizations (NGOs), including Church Action on Poverty, Christian Aid, Tear Fund, and CAFOD make particularly powerful contributions.[2] Such Christian and ethical initiatives are reminders that any consideration of prosperity and poverty in an urban context has to address not just the means of economic exchange, but also increasingly the purpose of economic life.

4.6   Christian tradition in Britain has increasingly focused attention on the common good of all, a rich concept drawing on a variety of faith traditions. The recent ecumenical report, *Prosperity with a Purpose*, particularly demonstrates this. The challenge we face, the Commission believes, is how to pursue a prosperity that brings human fulfilment for all – including the marginalized. The Commission is clear that by solely harnessing the values of status, power and profit, the fulfilment of all cannot be achieved.

4.7   This has important implications for the churches' contribution to economic debate. While the churches will continue to work in partnership with government, civil society, business and other faiths, they will be increasingly critical of theories and practices based purely on economics. They will also seek alternatives for the sake of the common good. The Church has firsthand, daily experience of the damage caused by severe poverty and inequality. Equally, the Church has firsthand experience of how significant wealth does not translate into significant happiness.

Growth and exclusion

4.8   There is a central ethical problem in modern economics: while prosperity is promoted through the justifiable route of economic growth (promoting well-being individually and collectively) such new prosperity is giving rise to grave inequalities. This is linked to the wider issue of global inequalities, both between nations and between individuals, because increasing global prosperity has been associated with increasing divisions between the richest and the poorest.

4.9   Prosperity is demonstrably associated with acute social divisions. For example, in terms of the distribution of income: in 2003-04, the original income (before taxes and benefits) of the top fifth of households in the UK was around 17 times greater than that of the bottom fifth (£63,200 per household per year compared with £3,700). After adjusting for taxes and benefits, this ratio was reduced to four to one for final income, unchanged from previous years.

Household income

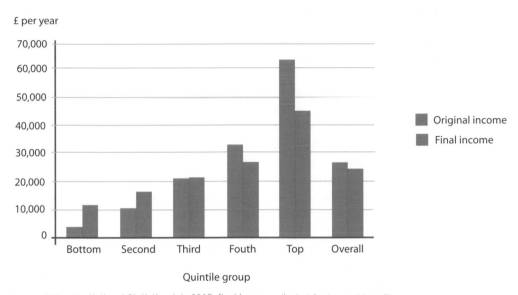

£ per year

Original income
Final income

Quintile group

Source: Office for National Statistics July 2005, final income adjusted for tax and benefits

4.10   Recent statistics show that, despite a large package of redistributive measures, the net effect of seven years of Labour government is to leave inequality effectively unchanged.

Income inequality

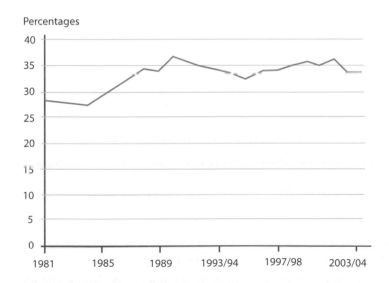

Percentages

No consistent trend since start of 1990s

Gini coefficient[3] for equivalized disposable income, UK

4.11   During the second half of the 1980s, income inequality had been increasing but inequality in disposable income has shown no consistent trend since the start of the 1990s. Inequality in original income (before taking account of taxes and benefits) increased fairly steadily throughout the 1980s but has also remained relatively stable since then. The Institute for Fiscal Studies (IFS)[4] has investigated some of the possible explanations for this higher level of inequality since the start of the 1980s:

- There has been an increase in wage inequality, and particularly an increase in the gap between wages for skilled and unskilled workers. Suggested reasons include skills-biased technological change and a decline in the role of trade unions. Growth in self-employment income and in unemployment was also found to be associated with periods of increased inequality.

- There has also been a decrease in the rate of male participation in the labour market, often in households where there is no other earner. There has also been increased female participation among those with working partners. This has led to an increased polarization between two-earner and zero-earner households, although in the late 1990s there was some fall in the proportion of people in workless households.

- Demographic factors, such as the growth in one person households, make a relatively unimportant contribution compared with labour market changes.

4.12   The IFS has found that the income tax cuts of the late 1980s worked to increase income inequality, while direct tax rises in the early 1990s – together with the increases in means-tested benefits in the late 1990s – produced the opposite effect. Overall, there has been only limited success in reducing poverty. In 2003–04, almost two-thirds of the population had incomes below the national average income of £408 per week. The distribution is skewed by a relatively small number of people on relatively high incomes. In 2003–04, half the population had household income of less than £336 per week. [5]

4.13   Despite the UK unemployment rate falling to 4.7% in 2005, around the lowest for 30 years, lack of work continues to be a major cause of poverty. Significantly this is concentrated in particularly deprived communities such as Knowsley in Merseyside and Merthyr Tydfil in South Wales. In addition – between the early 1980s and mid-1990s – there was a trebling of those dependent on Incapacity Benefits (long-term sick and disabled). The Government's drive to encourage claimants back to work has reduced the annual inflows to these benefits by around 30% since the mid-1990s. Nevertheless, the total number of incapacity benefit claimants in May 2005 stood at 2.78 million [6] and, in some wards, the numbers can reach 28% of the population.

4.14   The persistence of deep regional inequalities only exacerbates urban inequalities. The further you go from London, the gap widens between the poor communities in poor urban areas and the richer. This chronic inequality between those living in close proximity to one another, and continuing deprivation is as serious as the persistence of grave child poverty. It is one of the most startling findings of this Commission that 8 million (15%) of our fellow citizens are contained within the 10% of the poorest wards in the country.

How does Britain compare with the rest of Europe?

4.15   Inequality in Britain is well above average compared to all western nations based on 2001 figures. [7] Eurostat (the Statistical Office of the European Communities) shows that in the UK the ratio of total income received by the highest earning 20% of the population to that received by the 20% with the lowest income in the UK is one of the highest in Europe – well above the European average, based on the 2001 data.

The effects of inequalities

4.16   One fact that cannot be avoided is that the greater the inequality – measured in purely economic terms, between the highest paid and lowest paid, within any given nation or community – the greater the number of disaffected people of *every* economic status there will be.[8]

4.17   The ramifications of such differences for health and education opportunities are alarming. For example, the lack of affordable reliable transport can restrict access to work, education, services, food shopping and cultural activities. The growth of car use has in many ways exacerbated problems for those who cannot afford a car. They have to rely mainly on buses, which can be expensive, inconvenient and unreliable.

4.18   The greatest challenge facing secular capitalism[10] is how to generate greater prosperity while reducing the stubborn persistence of that deprivation which significantly disenfranchises people and communities from participating effectively in the mainstream of society's life. Urban communities bear a massively disproportionate burden of such poverty. The Commission therefore asserts that engagement with inequality continues to be the litmus test of the moral adequacy of any society. And for Christians, likewise, the commitment to the common good of all means we must be biased towards inclusion.

4.19   In the 1980s, *Faith in the City* faced up to the arguments over the nature and extent of poverty in a modern economy at the end of the age of industrialization. As that economy has advanced into the post-industrial age, the circumstances of the struggles of deprived urban communities may have changed, but not their nature. One adviser to the present Commission, who has lived in such communities all his life, said, 'Never have I seen such deprivation and loss of soul.' He was talking not about British urban priority areas in 1985, but about priority need estates in 2005.

> 'There must come a point at which the scale of the gap between the very wealthy and those at the bottom of the range of income begins to undermine the common good. This is the point at which society starts to be run for the benefit of the rich, not for all its members.' [9]

South Oxhey – 'island of deprivation'   [B4.1]

South Oxhey, near Watford, Hertfordshire has been described as 'an island of deprivation in a sea of prosperity'. In many ways it is exactly like any other large, deprived estate but it is distinctly different in that it sits in one of the most prosperous areas in the country. South Oxhey is an island. The estate was built after the war to house overcrowded Londoners and the victims of bombing. However, during the initial public enquiry in 1944 the surrounding local residents demanded that the estate must be invisible from any direction. It still is. It is surrounded by thick woods which hide it and separate it from all its wealthy neighbouring areas. There is no signpost to South Oxhey until you are actually about to enter the estate. Being hidden and surrounded by woods and wealth has, almost certainly, had an impact on the lives and self-image of those who live on the estate. There is much material poverty but there is a much greater poverty of spirit. There is a common perception in South Oxhey that nearby communities deride the residents of the estate, that, 'They think we are scum.'

At the heart of this close but isolated community lies All Saints' Church Centre. The modern building is designed for outreach and mission to the surrounding community and it is a place of comfort and refuge to the many deprived and struggling people who walk through its doors every day. The people of All Saints work hard to support and care for the most disadvantaged by providing for basic needs such as hot meals, company, furniture and household goods and any DIY skills we can offer.

The South Oxhey Christmas tree – 'the local vicar explains that it is surrounded by a huge fence to stop vandalism'

The dark (sea) side

The problem of low esteem and marginalization affects those in coastal communities too. These quotations come from a 24-hour conference on coastal communities initiated by the Commission.

'Coastal communities are unfashionable so they don't get the attention of other cities or towns. These communities have difficulty attracting key workers as often their partners can not get jobs, and even if they do they often feel isolated as they are the only professional. Being on the edge causes huge problems, including attracting leading people into local authorities and health authorities, and the quality of councillors and officers. The communities are often ill-served by the local authorities as their own local councillor fails to get heard or is voted down by the majority. Poverty of community expectations is a huge issue.'

Bishop David Rossdale from Lincolnshire

'People come to coastal towns with problems, but the problems can't go any further so they just wait there. There are just collections of large groups of dysfunctional people but they don't pass through, they just get stuck. There is a lot of escapism to the coastal resort. There are casual jobs in the summer but people just don't fit in. However, they still stay. But this could also happen on an inner-city estate. Being on the margins on an inner-city estate is just the same as being on the margins on the coast. Although similar to London housing estates, there is a feeling of isolation and enclosure, but coastal communities are more isolated because they are more on the edge.

Now we have the drugs scene, social breakdown, dysfunctional families and a real underclass who have no investment whatsoever in society. Coastal communities or coastal areas, which were once the places of beacons of hope, now share the same problems as urban areas, but their remoteness makes it worse.'

Venerable Tim Ellis, then Archdeacon of Stow and Lindsey

As journalist Polly Toynbee observed when she experienced living on low pay for a period: 'Wherever I walked, everything I passed was out of bounds, things belonging to other people but not to me. No Starbucks sofas beckoned any more, no Borders bookshop, no restaurants, not even the most humble café. This is what exclusion means, if you ever wondered at this wider definition of poverty. It is a large No Entry sign on every ordinary pleasure. No Entry to the consumer society where the rest of us live. It is a harsh apartheid.'[12]

4.20 There is significant consensus among policy makers, academia and church leaders, that the kind of deprivation experienced in modern urban Britain involves the 'loss of access to the most important life chances that a modern society offers, where those chances connect individuals to the mainstream of life in that society'. This marginalization both generates and is informed by a lack of self-worth: 'The worst blow of all is the contempt of your fellow citizens', a contempt fuelled by the media and other social structures, which essentially promote 'the Othering of people in society'.[11]

4.21 Churches must, by their own teaching, preaching and practice, demonstrate the gospel challenge to the rich – wealth brings obligations to those who are less fortunate and these obligations go beyond simply paying tax. The churches need to add their own confident voice to the public recognition that there is an unacceptable gap between rich and poor in Britain. This gap between rich and poor is offensive to the Christian gospel. Judeo-Christian teaching is not against the wealthy, but it does require that we make a stern challenge to those who are rich but ignore the needs of the poor. The churches must communicate this message to comfortable Britain, where even though most people might not count themselves as wealthy – in reality we and they have more than enough.

A living wage

4.22 While the introduction of a minimum wage (£5.05 per hour from October 2005) and the Working Families Tax Credit has improved the living standards of lower-paid families with children, many still remain in poverty. In Manchester, for example, 17% of vacancies and 52% of part-time vacancies paid below the lower earnings limit. Workers taking these jobs would not be entitled to any contributory social security benefits. Many of the jobs provide a low level of weekly income and workers would not be independent of benefit and tax credits.

4.23   While higher earners' salaries have risen by 60% over 20 years, wages for the lowest paid workers have barely increased at all.[13] They may live cheek by jowl in the modern city, but their lives barely intersect.

4.24   Life on a minimum wage can also render people more vulnerable to poverty. Local markets, for example, have a tendency to work to the advantage of the rich. The National Consumer Council has documented how people in poverty pay more for a range of goods and services within the market – in particular for utilities such as energy, water and telephones. There are a number of reasons for this. If you are on a low income, you may be stuck with expensive payment methods and supplies; you may need to use more of the utilities than most, and there is no incentive for providers to design services that benefit low-income consumers.

4.25   Yet the working poor outnumber unemployed people or poor pensioners. People may work hard for long hours, but in the absence of a living wage, they still fall below the poverty line. This development is particularly significant, not least because of government policy to encourage people to move from benefits into employment.

4.26   When local faith and community leaders have decided to raise with statutory bodies issues that are not sanctioned or on the official agenda, they can meet with hostility. The East London Communities Organization found this in its Living Wage campaign. The campaign sought the introduction of an ethical contracting policy for cleaning, catering and other auxiliary services in East London's NHS. The aim was that the hundreds of workers doing these jobs would receive pay and conditions on a par with staff working in the same roles who were directly employed by the NHS.

4.27   The Strategic Health Authority and the individual hospital trusts of East London, who were the targets of this campaign, had published a number of aspirational documents committing to listen to local people, to being open to consultation and to working in partnership with the wider community for a healthier East London. Yet when the issue of wage justice was raised by a broad coalition of faith communities and unions, and the personal testimonies of contracted-out staff earning the national minimum wage were given a public airing, the managers and directors of the NHS Trusts reacted angrily and refused to recognize that this was a legitimate concern.

4.28   Only widespread publicity and sustained pressure forced the Trusts to discuss the problem, and to recognize the community and faith institutions that had brought it up. In the end a moderate but significant deal was hammered out to bring contract staff onto parity with NHS conditions over three years. Reaching an agreement restored people's faith that it is possible to successfully seek and win change.

Household debt

4.29   The growth in household debt among low-income families is another concern. These people, with no savings to speak of, are vulnerable to any kind of crisis or unexpected item of expenditure. The rapidly growing indebtedness of the British (the Citizens Advice Bureau reported a 47% growth in debt problems 1998–2003) is particularly damaging for the poor. They are marginalized from access to cheaper credit shared by the rest of the population. Eight million people are refused access to mainstream credit, and 3 million are driven to borrowing regularly from doorstep lenders, charging up to 200% APR.

4.30   A community survey on Meadowell estate, North Shields, by the church-based Cedarwood Trust, found that, out of 142 households, 87% were paying doorstep lenders an average of 33.5% of their total weekly income. Families were paying

'Chambermaids, often in top-class hotels, may be contracted to work at an hourly rate equivalent to the minimum wage but the number of rooms they are required to clean and prepare are far too many to be done in one hour resulting in the women having to work far longer than they are contracted to do.'

'I work as a cleaner/porter in a hospital. I worked 36½ hours last week, and after tax etc., my take-home pay was £131.'
Belfast worker

£66 per week out of a total income of £200. Single people had to find £27 out of a total of £82. Interest rates ranged from 33% to 2000%.

4.31 The impact of high levels of debt at extortionate rates of interest on families who are already struggling on inadequate incomes can be particularly severe. In the words of a woman who attended a Church Action on Poverty Policy Forum on debt in 2001:

> 'I have a 15-year-old daughter and she needs clothes, so I have to get a Provi loan or vouchers. It's hard. At the end of my benefit I've nothing left to pay back the loan and vouchers. I can't spend money on shopping and bills.'

'Obtaining credit is an essential part of everyday life for people on low incomes. 90% of people needed to borrow money not only to buy essential items, but also to make ends meet. People regularly borrowed to pay bills, to buy clothes and school uniforms, and for birthdays, holidays and Christmas – often out of sheer desperation.'[14]

Escape from debt [B4.3]

The Meadowell Estate in North Tyneside has undergone a makeover since it was hit by riots ten years ago. But poverty is still widespread and that means that, for many, debt is a problem. It is estimated that doorstep lenders collect over £10,000 a week from families on the estate. The Cedarwood Trust is a church-linked pastoral care organization helping people cope with life on low incomes. Cedarwood offers help with debt in partnership with the Citizens Advice Bureaux (CAB). Through a credit union it enables local people to both save and borrow and escape from the door-to-door market with its high cost loans. The Cedarwood Trust, under the guidance of Margaret Nolan, has also been active in the campaign to persuade the Government to take action against loan sharks. With the support of Church Action on Poverty and the 'Debt on your Doorstep' campaign, the Department of Trade and Industry has been persuaded to fund research into the possibility of capping the interest rates that door-to-door loan companies can charge.

'But,' as Margaret Nolan explains, 'the pressure on the Government, based on the hard-won experience and research of the Cedarwood Trust and other initiatives like it, will not stop until there is a change in the law and extortionate interest rates are no longer a hazard for poor communities.'

Growing globalization

4.32 The increasing marketization of life generates great benefits but it is undeniable that it incurs grave costs which bear down particularly on the poor. The historic problem of the free market economy is now being enacted on a global scale.

4.33 The necessity to be more competitive in the global economy, through promoting deregulation, liberalized trading, and privatization, can have the effect of further undermining the very fragile existence of deprived urban people and communities. Government invokes social capital as the glue to hold society together, yet those same global pressures work their way into the fabric of the local community, eroding that social capital. This in turn contributes to an erosion of relationships, of justice and of peace. In the end it is the poor who are most damaged.

4.34 The marginalization of Britain's poor, especially the growth of the unskilled and unqualified working poor, will be made worse as China and India take advantage of globalization. Their comparative advantage rests on a massive labour force which Britain's already marginalized urban communities cannot compete with. That plight will be heightened by the growing power of highly paid executives, operating across national boundaries, with less and less loyalty to any particular place.

4.35 Those experiencing poverty are further undermined by being confined in enclosed urban spaces. In Britain, the 'ghettos' of the rich and the poor are increasingly visible, spatially and architecturally, and they represent a fault line connecting Britain's marginalized with those in the less developed economies of the world. This growing global inequality makes it far more costly and difficult to create more just and cohesive societies for the common good of all.

4.36 The indisputable contribution of *economic capital* to prosperity is accompanied by a damaging erosion of those personal virtues (such as trust), and the public benefits (such as collective provision for all), of *social capital* and the damage done to the environment. The pursuit of prosperity risks creating such an acquisitive global society that the only values that count are profit, power and status. Such a pursuit of prosperity raises moral questions – essentially a critique of economic capitalism by faithful capital. But Christians need to practise what they preach, which has not always been the case.

Including those who suffer deprivation in the debate

4.37 One of the obstacles to creating the political will to tackle structural poverty and inequality is the tendency for public opinion to be shaped by stereotypes rather than the facts. These are often fuelled by media portrayals of people experiencing poverty as ignorant and lazy, the suggestion that poor people only have themselves to blame and that there are jobs out there if you can be bothered to look for them. Professor Ruth Lister recently described this in terms of the 'Othering' of people in poverty.[15]

Failure to listen

4.38 Set against this is the increasing geographical and social invisibility of those who experience poverty, who lack an organized political voice and are increasingly disengaged from the political process. In a society where the focus is on glamour and celebrity, the poor become invisible and unheard. Could this be because poverty tends disproportionately to affect women, children, the elderly, the sick and disabled, and ethnic minorities?

4.39 But government and others must listen to the voices and perspectives of peoples' own experiences of poverty. Their attitudes and ideas about what can be done to tackle poverty, and the stories of their resilience amidst adversity, must be valued and understood in today's society.

4.40 In 2001, the Commission on Poverty, Participation and Power reported on the anger and frustration of those experiencing poverty who believe their voices are not being heard.[17]

4.41 It isn't enough to engage in projects on behalf of those facing urban poverty and social exclusion. Our Commission would like to see those people brought to the fore of the debate, and the Government must find alternative ways of engaging with those suffering from inequalities.

Learning from the developing world

4.42 The Government works to achieve this in their programmes for the developing world, and must consider whether similar approaches – such as the Sustainable Living Programme – could be adopted here.

4.43 How policy makers respond to poverty determines how we understand poverty. There has been a tendency in both the Northern and Southern hemispheres to view urban people in poverty as monochrome and passive. Perhaps we can learn from the experiences developed by those working in international development where the philosophy has shifted from a 'top down' paternalistic approach to one which pays closer attention to the expressed needs of poor communities. In particular, the Commission commends what has become known as the Sustainable Livelihoods Approach,[18] which takes as its starting point not deprivation but the 'wealth of the poor'[19]:

4.44 Sustainable Livelihoods approach to poverty and community regeneration, commonplace in the developing world, turns many of our notions of what communities need upside down. Instead of defining an area by what it lacks, and by a set of depressing statistics, a Sustainable Living (SL) approach looks at the assets and strengths within a community. With detailed mapping and research,

'People in poverty are not asked how they want to be described. This is symptomatic of a failure to listen to what they have to say about the meaning of poverty. Lack of respect, denial of dignity and a consequent sense of shame and worthlessness are constant refrains when people in poverty talk about how they are treated. Two contributions at a national hearing held by Church Action on Poverty are representative: "The worst blow of all is the contempt of your fellow citizens. I and many families live in that contempt"; and "I just feel very angry sometimes that people are ignorant of the fact that we are humans as well and we do need to be respected".'[16]

it then aims to unblock barriers and create opportunities for developing such strengths and assets. Solutions will focus on changing systems and cultures, and relate as much to re-allocating existing resources, as to looking for new ones. The Sustainable Living approach is slower, is directed by grassroots local people, and, as its name, suggests is longer term.

4.45   The Sustainable Living concept allows local people the dignity of being able to define their situation for themselves rather than being labelled by others. The model offers a holistic, radical understanding of community regeneration based upon some core values of human worth, identity, and ways of relating to each other in contrast to many of the more mechanistic notions (such as outputs) which have recently defined regeneration initiatives. So the Sustainable Living approach invites a different way of understanding the way things are – and how they might be changed – based on local people's experience and the ways they have found of surviving and sustaining ways of living. Church Action on Poverty and Oxfam are pioneering the first systematic Sustainable Living model in the small town of Thornaby on Tees.

4.46   Income, whether from paid employment or state benefit, is a vital factor in people's livelihoods but there are many more sources of 'capital', from social networks, education and personal skills to access to transport. All of these, working together, determine whether a livelihood is sustainable. Equally important, is the interaction between individuals and households and wider institutional structures and processes.

4.47   At a practical level, this means that the Sustainable Living approach:

■ Starts with an analysis of people's livelihoods and their methods of coping;
■ Fully involves people and respects their views;
■ Focuses on the impact of different policy and institutional arrangements upon people and their households as well as the areas of their lives that they consider are affected by poverty;
■ Emphasizes that influencing these policies and institutional arrangements must include the participation of the poor and promote their agenda;
■ Works to support people to achieve their own livelihood goals.

Participatory budgeting – community decision making

4.48   The Commission also believes that 'participatory budgeting' offers a viable way of developing community involvement in decision making. Manchester Pride, with the support of Church Action on Poverty and the Oxfam UK Poverty Programme, has pioneered participatory budgeting involving a range of stakeholders and Salford City Council. As a result, there is now growing interest in participatory budgeting from local government councils throughout the UK. The long-term potential of participatory budgeting is huge as it enables those who are usually marginalized to enter the debate and participate in decisions about public expenditure that affect their communities.

Gaining the whole world . . .

4.49 There is a deeper and still more troubling question about capitalism than simply outlining the ways in which it promotes inequality. It is time to question whether this economic and social model can really promote the happiness or well-being of all.

4.50 As we have already said, the story of the British economy from 1950 to the present is of economic growth averaging 2.5% a year. Since *Faith in the City* was published in the 1980s, there has been almost continuous economic growth, with record numbers in employment, the lowest rate of unemployment for around 30 years, and growing personal prosperity.

4.51 In tandem with this, increasing consumption and greater disposable income saw 41.2 million holidays taken abroad in 2003 – a sixfold increase from 1971. With more than half of British households now having access to the internet and online shopping booming, perhaps it is no surprise that three-quarters of Britons say they have no material comforts missing from their lives. And living standards projected to increase by 35% from 1998 to 2010. But does all this materialism make us happy?

4.52 Richard Layard [22] argues that increasing standards of living in advanced economies like Britain, as measured by increasing GNP per head, has *not* resulted in increasing happiness. Using 1970 as a base, GNP per capita increased significantly by 1997. However, the proportion of people describing themselves as happy did not match this increase, but instead remained constant. In nations where an individual's average income is over $15,000, Layard has found that increasing economic growth per capita did not produce increasing happiness. But for nations below that figure, increases in economic growth were met with increasing happiness.

4.53 This suggests that, above a certain level of income, any increase in prosperity is unlikely to generate an equivalent increase in happiness. 'That is the challenge and the paradox', concludes Layard.

Participatory budgeting: a World Bank explanation [B4.5

Participatory budgeting is a process by which a wide range of stakeholders debate, analyse, prioritize, and monitor decisions about public expenditures and investments. Participatory budgeting can occur in three different stages of public expenditure management:

- *Budget formulation and analysis. Citizens participate in allocating budgets according to priorities they have identified in participatory poverty diagnostics; formulate alternate budgets; or assess proposed allocations in relation to a government's policy commitments and stated concerns and objectives.*
- *Expenditure monitoring and tracking. Citizens track whether public spending is consistent with allocations made in the budget and track the flow of funds to the agencies responsible for the delivery of goods and services.*
- *Monitoring of public service delivery. Citizens monitor the quality of goods and services provided by government in relation to expenditures made for these goods and services, a process similar to citizen report cards or scorecards.*

Increased participation in budgeting can lead to the formulation of and investment in pro-poor policies, greater societal consensus, and support for difficult policy reforms. Experiences with participatory budgeting have shown positive links between participation, sound macro-economic policies, and more effective government. Participatory budgeting processes have been utilized in a number of different countries, including Ireland, Canada, India, Uganda, Brazil, and South Africa.[23]

GDP and Life Satisfaction

A CHALLENGE TO THE ECONOMIC STATUS QUO

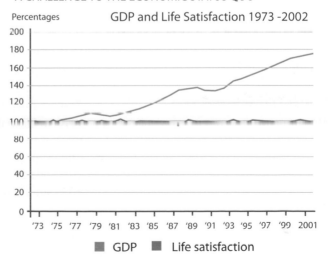

Percentages   GDP and Life Satisfaction 1973 -2002

■ GDP ■ Life satisfaction

Source: New Economics Foundation

The well-being of young people

4.54   One of the key barriers to childhood happiness and to future prospects is growing up in a poor household. Child poverty rose during the 1980s and early 1990s and by the late 1990s the UK had the highest child poverty rate in the EU. Since 1998–99, the number of children living in low-income households (before housing costs) has fallen from 3.1 million to 2.5 million and the number living in low-income households (after housing costs) has fallen from 4.1 million to 3.5 million.[24]

4.55   However, evidence suggests that children from prosperous homes are also unhappy. Research[25] undertaken by the Commission shows that:

- 70% of urban young people felt that life was really worth living and 56% felt that their lives had a sense of purpose.
- On the other hand, 52% often felt depressed and 27% said that they had sometimes considered suicide.
- When young people had problems, they were more likely to find it helpful to talk to their friends (64%) than to their mother (50%) or their father (32%).[26]
- 28% were worried about being bullied at school.
- Almost three-quarters (74%) of urban young people liked living in their local area. However, only a minority (20%) felt that their area cared about young people. Moreover, substantial proportions of young people (between 26% and 48%) were concerned about growing vandalism, crime, violence, drug-taking and drinking in their area.

4.56   Government statistics also show that we are not supporting our young people to cope with the pressures of life[27]:

- In 2004, 1 in 10 children in Great Britain aged 5 to 16 had a clinically recognizable mental disorder. This was the same as the proportion recorded in the 1999 survey.
- Boys were more likely than girls to have a mental disorder. Among 5- to 10-year-olds, 10% of boys and 5% of girls had a mental disorder. Among 11- to 16-year-olds, the proportions were 13% for boys and 10% for girls.
- It was greater among children in lone-parent families (16% per) than among those in two-parent families (8%), and in families with neither parent working (20%) compared with those in which both parents worked (8%).
- In 2001/02, among young people (those aged 16 to 24), 35% of men and 24% of women said that they had taken an illicit drug in the previous year. The drug most commonly used by young people was cannabis.[28]
- Since 1996 there has been an increase in the use of cocaine among young people, especially among young men.
- In 2003, nearly one in three adults (31%) had exceeded the recommended daily alcohol intake (of 4 units for men and 3 for women) on at least one day during the previous week.[29]
- Young drinkers aged 11 to 15 in England doubled their average weekly consumption of alcohol during the 1990s – from 5.3 in 1990 to 10.4 units in 2004. It has since stabilized for boys and continues to increase for girls. The greatest increase has been among girls aged 14, from 3.8 units in 1992 to 9.7 in 2004. In each year, among those who drank, boys consumed more alcohol than girls in every age group.
- The proportion of children who drank increased with age, from 4 % of 11-year-olds to 45% of 15-year-olds in 2004. Among both boys and girls, 23% aged 11 to 15 drank alcohol in the previous week.[30]

Alcohol consumption

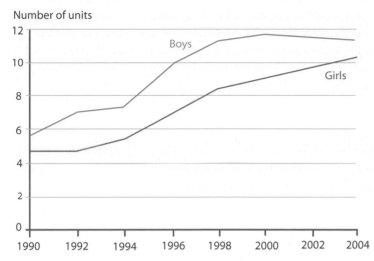

Number of units

Mean alcohol consumption of children aged 11-15 who drank in the last week, by sex, England, 1990-2004

4.57 The World Health Organization's survey on young people in 2004[31] found that young people in Britain were among the most depressed in Europe.

4.58 Government, the Church and others need to take this seriously. We need to work with young people to find ways to help them cope with the pressures of life and we must make investment in young people a priority.

4.59 In the sphere of education, some re-focusing is required, away from the more performance-driven models to the development of informal and holistic educational approaches which incorporate mind, body and emotions. As the Archbishop of Canterbury Dr Rowan Williams has said, too much of our schooling is based on 'an educational philosophy which is obsessed with testing. It's another form of our obsession with results and productivity and it's a particularly malign one in a context where, if we are trying to educate persons, we ought to be educating in emotional and communicative literacy as well as in other kinds of literacy'.[32] With this in mind, our Commission believes that the proper funding of the statutory youth service would help develop confidence and accountability. Such an act would signal the importance of informal education and its capacity to transform young people – helping them to gain their full potential alongside more formal school curricula. There must be better incentives to recruit and retain youth workers, for example by giving them key worker status.

4.60 The Commission's research shows that those young people with a sense of purpose are more resilient to the pressures of living in the twenty-first century and are more likely to possess the positive aspects of young people's well-being.[33]

4.61 We recommend that all professionals working with young people are alert to the different approaches to helping young people develop a sense of purpose and are encouraged to adopt them in their practice.

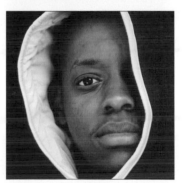

4.62 It is also important to listen to young people from all backgrounds in shaping policies and practice. Therefore, churches, local authorities, police and other statutory authorities should hold local forums or consultations with young people on a regular basis so that their views can help shape the authorities' strategic planning and to help inform an assessment of what is working and not working in the local community.

4.63 Faced with such evidence of misery in a prosperous Britain, we need to challenge both economic and government policy that does not recognize that there is a purpose to life beyond economic growth. Would following an alternative path reduce the inequalities as well as make us happier?

4.64 For the Churches' urban economic agenda a number of matters arise.

Happiness may indeed depend on much more than increasing purchasing power, but the issue of growing real income remains central to government policy. This has important implications for developing adequate individual basic income levels, significantly through paid employment. Layard's contention that happiness depends significantly on work of any kind is understandable, but his recognition of the importance of achieving a basic income for individuals has other implications. It means that incomes should be enough to reduce inequalities globally and nationally - again linked to increasing world basic income levels to the minimum for human fulfilment ($15,000 a head per year).

4.65   However, in addition to achieving such basic income/ employment and greater equality between incomes, there is now a growing recognition that other factors are also essential for human happiness:

- Happier and fulfilled, not richer and depressed
- Fulfilled and secure relations in personal life
- Relations that spread beyond personal to create good community life and relationships
- Good health, especially mental health
- Freedom, including the scope to participate in matters affecting one's life
- A philosophy of life, including a commitment to something beyond the individual

4.66   A second study into happiness by Dr Martin Seligman[34] has identified that there are three levels of happiness:

- **The Pleasant Life:** satisfying the visceral pleasures of the body such as having a glass of good wine, a hot bath or a walk in the park. Such pleasures are transitory and superficial and cannot produce true well-being, but they can make life enjoyable for a moment.
- **The Good Life:** engaging in activity, often social in nature, which causes vigorous enjoyment through a challenge - say, playing Sunday football or going to a book club.
- **The Meaningful Life:** the highest level of sustained happiness comes when people can give a wider meaning to their lives. Helping others through politics, voluntary work or religion can help people to realize that there is something bigger and more important than themselves.

4.67   Martin Seligman has found that those who pursue all three lives, pleasure, engagement, and meaning, have by far the most life satisfaction, with engagement and meaning contributing far and away the most to fulfilment.

4.68   The Government has recognized the benefits of volunteering and should be commended for its efforts to get people engaged, for example, through the Year of the Volunteer. However, government needs to see volunteering as more than just service delivery. The benefits are huge.

Challenges ahead

4.69   In 2000, local councils gained the power to promote economic, social and environmental well-being, and the New Economics Foundation - recognizing that despite our economic prosperity we do not necessarily feel happier with our lives - is developing a well-being programme (see below). But many are not facing up to the emerging implications.

4.70   Over its two-year deliberation, the Commission was struck, with the approach taken by the New Economics Foundation.[35] Its 'well-being manifesto for a flourishing society', challenges the assumption that growing the economy is government's most important function.

A well-being manifesto

[B4.6

The New Economics Foundation's manifesto[36] calls on government to help UK citizens be happier and more fulfilled – not richer and more depressed. It offers a number of suggestions for how government could promote well-being, including:

- *Measure what matters, for example, by producing a set of national well-being accounts which look at how we feel about and how engaged we are with the society and environment in which we live.*

- *Create a well-being economy – high-quality work can affect our well-being by providing us with purpose, challenge, and opportunities for social relationships.*

- *Reclaim our time by increasing flexible working provision, introducing more bank holidays and reducing the working week because spending time with our children, families and friends and communities brings us more happiness.*

- *Create an education system that promotes flourishing which will enable young people to realize their potential and enable them to become capable and emotionally well-rounded as well as happy and motivated. Schools therefore need to have a strategy to promote emotional, social, spiritual and physical well-being.*

- *Refocus the health system to promote complete health, defined by the World Health Organization as 'a state of complete physical, mental and social well-being and not merely the absence of disease or infirmity'.*

- *Invest in the very early years and parenting – cost benefit analysis shows that investment in the age group zero to three repays itself many times over, due to reduced health, education and social costs in the future. Parents need to be actively supported in order to become the best parents they can be.*

- *Discourage materialism and promote authentic advertising: promoting materialism is not only bad for the environment but also undermines well-being. People need to increase time spent in sports centres, arts venues and parks and reduce time shopping and watching TV.*

- *Strengthen civil society, social well-being and active citizenship: being actively engaged with communities has been shown not only to give us a personal sense of well-being but also has a positive knock-on effect for others.*

4.71   The New Economics Foundation has produced the first UK Measure of Domestic Progress (MDP) towards sustainable development. The MDP is an adjusted economic measure of the kind proposed in the US by former World Bank economist Herman Daly. It builds on over a decade of work to define such indicators in a number of different countries.

4.72   The UK index adjusts personal consumer expenditure to account for a variety of economic, environmental and social factors not included in the GDP. For example, the MDP adds in the benefits of household labour, accounts for income inequality, subtracts social costs (such as crime, traffic congestion, family breakdown) and environmental costs (such as air pollution, resource depletion and the 'hidden' costs of climate change) and makes adjustments for long-term investment and economic sustainability.

Prosperity and equity

4.73   A strong economy without equity is unjust and arguably, ultimately unsustainable. It also fails to deliver life satisfaction and well-being to those for whom the system works.

4.74   Pursuing sustainable growth with equity would mean the Government should consider using a wider measure of sustainable growth than GDP, for example, the NEF's measure of domestic progress or indices such as the Index of Sustainable Economic Welfare. [37] The Audit Commission's quality of life indicators [38] are a good start, but need to be built on because they are weak on social well-being.

4.75   Despite political and economic constraints, the Government does face key strategic choices in order to balance continued growth and economic stability with wider social and political objectives and tackle poverty and inequality.

4.76   Grave inequalities in health, education, housing, culture and income have to be addressed as such inequalities have proven damaging effects on communities. The greater the inequalities, the more expensive it is to improve the position of the poor. This has profound implications for UK Government policies. If they do not effectively address this obstacle, then we face severe limits on any likelihood of reducing urban deprivation, and therefore improving the prosperity and well-being of all our citizens.

4.77   The choices ahead, however, are not simply matters of economic or political calculation. They are fundamentally moral choices about the kind of twenty-first-century society we wish to live in. But will those with power, profit and status be willing to make the right choices for the common good of all?

5 Regeneration for People:
More than Status, Power and Profit

5.1   The face of urban Britain is changing faster and more dramatically than at any time in living memory. But to what extent do the people who live in the city have any say in the kind of changes that are underway? It is a central premise of our Commission that the political culture and habits of our cities must be ones that sustain human flourishing, and that a well-populated public life is essential for good governance in our town and cities. But how does national and local government hear the voice of its people when a 'democratic deficit' is acknowledged by all political parties and institutions? And does a democratic vacuum allow the values of status, power, profit and security to dominate the agenda of urban regeneration?

5.2   In the last 20 years Britain has witnessed a widespread decline in associational life and traditional forms of political participation.[2] Yet while membership of most churches has followed this trend, we have found that many local church communities, alongside congregations of other faiths, stand out in urban localities as among the most vibrant institutions in civil society.

5.3   This is not to deny the difficulties that urban congregations face in building and sustaining community, not least, a highly mobile population – but their many qualities, including deep local roots, are a source of strength and courage to members and leaders. And if, as we have seen in earlier chapters, migration has presented challenges in our cities in recent years, it has also sustained and reinvigorated many faith communities. The reality of urban poverty, and of migration, keeps local congregations very close to the tensions in cities and towns which arise from people's struggle for housing and jobs, for places at good schools and for recognition in general.

5.4   Change in the political context of urban areas, and in faith communities themselves, requires a fresh look at the role of congregations in the public life of British cities and urban areas. We see a vibrant and strategically significant role for local congregations in civic life, not least in speaking up and taking action for social and economic justice. We recognize the many challenges that congregations face in working for change in the world around them, but we have no doubt that a properly resourced and planned approach by faith communities to equipping their people for civic participation would make a real difference to the quality of life in our cities. Communities of faith in urban Britain are in a unique position to develop creative and dignified solutions, at a local level, to the varied problems in our cities.

5.5   In the face of the 'democratic deficit', sustaining a healthy public realm is something with which churches and faith communities must be concerned – because it is the weakest and most vulnerable who lose most from an impoverished democratic life. Local congregations, along with other civil society organizations, can bring an energized ethical dimension to bear on the governance of our towns and cities. As Commissioners we found people hungry for a moral account of what makes a good city (see Chapter 6).

5.6   In recent years a regeneration 'industry' has been transforming the fabric of our poorest urban districts. Our interest – in the light of what people see happening to their neighbourhoods – is in examining the values that undergird these regeneration programmes, and asking whose interests they serve. We have also raised questions about the increasing political and commercial emphasis on security and order in urban areas. We have drawn on considerable evidence from people of faith who have participated in programmes of civil and neighbourhood renewal and we have also looked at changes taking place in public services, particularly with the invitation to faith communities to become involved in their delivery. (This is explored in more detail in Chapter 7.) The blurring of public and private interests in British life, particularly in our urban areas, is something about which people of faith have said relatively little, yet its implications for democratic accountability and fairness raise important moral questions.

New model cities and twenty-first-century urban regeneration

5.7   In the twenty-four hours between 6 and 7 July 2005, Londoners moved from celebrating a successful Olympic bid to witnessing the horror of suicide bombings on the public transport system. These contrasting events dramatically illuminate dynamics in urban Britain which we have sought to understand.

5.8   The Olympic Games, which come to London in 2012, are a trophy event among the sporting and cultural prizes for which cities compete, as part of the wider games of international competition. This competitive struggle between cities for prominence and profile is a challenge which civic and national leaders readily embrace. Ferocious marketing of cities to win these contests goes hand-in-hand with the appeal to global companies, and upwardly mobile individuals, to locate 'with us'. British cities are being significantly reshaped, and 'status, power, profit and security' appear to be the dominant values at work.

5.9   In the last ten years a multi-billion pound urban 'regeneration' industry has become an umbrella for cultural, environmental, retail, leisure, and housing development in urban Britain. It covers a great breadth of activities and provides huge salaries. For some, it is an ironic sign of how poverty can become big business. As the regeneration industry has expanded, religious groups have gained significant recognition in government and local authority policy. But if local faith leaders often feel overwhelmed by the demands and expectations placed on their involvement, they remain marginal players in the big economic competition around premier 'opportunity areas' such as the Thames Gateway.

5.10   Property is king in the regeneration game. The enhancement of real estate has become a centrepiece in 'the city's productive economy, an end in itself, justified by appeals to jobs, taxes and tourism'.[3] Inner-city gentrification, fuelled by an advertising driven media is a widespread phenomenon bringing dynamism, even glamour, to disadvantaged urban districts as property prices rocket. But all too often this phenomenon is about poorer populations being displaced and dispersed, with the middle class arriving to take residential control.[4] Even the 'affordable' component built into new urban developments is often considerably beyond the reach of people on low and insecure incomes, including many in work. The language of urban 'renaissance' has glossed over the less palatable by-products of property-driven economic development, while the human cost of rising property prices for those shut out of the bubble has received little public attention.

5.11   Churches have experienced these changes in different ways. Some have gentrified through the relocation of groups from wealthier parts of cities (church planting), others are left feeling marooned as populations change but not their congregation. Many older churches have benefited from the rise in property prices and have been able to realize assets for use elsewhere. At the same time, new Christian congregations and congregations of other faiths aiming to establish a permanent presence with a building, struggle to cover the inflated cost of property.

5.12   In London and other metropolitan centres, land adjacent to the 'waternet' (the network of tidal and non-tidal waterways) has a strong correlation with urban deprivation (see box B5.1).[5] Today, this is where the highest concentration of property-led economic development is taking place. Almost no one is asking whether the construction of one- and two-bedroom apartments, with high levels of security, overlooking canals is the form of local economic development best suited to assist the unemployed and lone parent families who live nearby.[6]

5.13   The regeneration industry works with a 'trickle-down' model, which assumes that the gentrification of poor areas, and the erection of shiny new buildings, public and private, will transform the fortunes of the deprived. This assumption is rarely tested in an open way – the political imperative to show big regeneration projects as successful is often just too strong.

London's Waternet

Fig 1

London's Opportunity

■ 20% most deprived wards
■ Development

—— The waternet

The civic role of faith communities

5.14   Local leaders of all faiths experience the impact of shifting economic opportunities, labour market dynamics and regeneration and development on their communities. They live with both the positive and negative effects of these changes on people and their families.

5.15   Occasionally, faith congregations in our urban areas find themselves in the eye of the storm in outbreaks of urban tension. While this chapter was being written, rioting broke out in the Lozells area of Birmingham between the African-Caribbean community and the area's mixed Asian communities – resulting in the death of an innocent man who worked for the city council, and in serious injuries for many others. The fighting erupted outside a Black-led church, where appeals for calm had been taking place. A short time later, mosque leaders in a neighbouring district of the city successfully prevented 300 angry youths from travelling to Lozells.

5.16   The intimacy of many faith congregations with the inevitable tensions arising from urban poverty means that, where they choose to become actively engaged with questions of social, economic and racial justice, they are in a particularly strong position to propose creative and effective solutions to community problems.

5.17   Whether this happens depends first on inclination and second on capability. Many local institutions of faith would rather not become embroiled in contentious questions of urban justice – their leaders encourage an inward-looking mentality and a tendency towards sectarianism. This exists in every faith and denomination. They have been described as 'the ecclesiastical equivalent to the gated communities which are proliferating . . . through gentrification'.[8]

These attitudes, sometimes fuelled by crude competition for worshippers, are a huge stumbling block to faith communities acting as agents of social cohesion, community harmony and indeed social justice.

5.18   Alternatively, the Commission found many examples of 'engagement by faith' in the public life of urban areas which involved one clergy-person sitting on a regeneration board or Local Strategic Partnership in significant isolation from the wider community. However dedicated individual ministers may be, allowing civic engagement by representatives of faith organizations to be left to one or two people is ultimately unhealthy. Furthermore, clergy are commonly overworked and imperfectly supported for this role.

5.19   The development and preparation of lay people, through their congregations, to speak up and take action for just change in urban areas deserves substantial additional investment by the churches, and by other faith communities. The Citizen Organizing Foundation offers one model. Hundreds of people each year from different local faith congregations (and from secular civil society organizations) spend several days together learning about each other, exploring areas of common concern in the challenging urban neighbourhoods where they live, and developing the skills and confidence to become active participants in the creation of change.[9] Another model being developed is the Core Cities Theology Network at the William Temple Foundation, which is bringing together 'in an environment of solidarity and support, those engaged in urban mission and public policy, so that more effective ways of being the church in the core cities context might be enabled'.[10]

5.20   Other local initiatives are also being developed that enable people to reflect on and act on their perception of the 'common good', in particular, the development of local ministry teams that have the potential to provide a structure that can carry discernment and the commitment of people from the wider neighbourhood and not just from church congregations.

'Ministering communities' in Gloucester   [B5.3]

In Gloucester Diocese, local congregations considering the development of local ministry teams, are encouraged to involve all the households in the parish. Every household in the neighbourhood is invited to nominate people they know whom they feel would be good at promoting the well-being of the community: i.e. those who have integrity, gifts and skills to lead and enable and encourage others in relation work 'for the common good' of a specific locality. Training and support to help groups engage with their various local contexts and personal appraisals are part of a package available to the local team as it endeavours to create 'ministering communities' in the neighbourhood.

The key questions that are reflected on by the groups are:
- *What can we celebrate and what is going well?*
- *What are the challenges we face?*
- *What do we choose to build on?*
- *What do we want to change?*

In the town of Painswick the local ministry team, working with other churches, twice called together local young people. At these forums the young people were asked about the issues they faced and their interests. Their greatest passion was sports. So a local charity was set-up (PSALMS - Painswick and Stroud Area Local Ministries) and within four months £77,000 had been raised for a sports-specialist youth minister working with the churches, a local school and a sports club.

5.21 The theologian William Cavanaugh urges the church to see itself as an 'alternative performance'. Unlike the 'performance' of the secular city, which understands human interests to be inherently competitive, the Christian performance should be based on an understanding of humans as created for 'mutual fellowship in God'. That is not to imply a wholly negative relationship to the state, or an automatic rejection of partnerships with statutory bodies. It is to suggest that such engagements require scrutiny of both their theological assumptions and practical effects.

5.22 Congregations and their leaders need an accurate understanding of the changing context in which they operate – and the impact of social and economic change on their mission. They also need practical examples of what 'alternative performance' involves. This may simply mean identifying how their existing practices form people and community in ways that challenge the dominant culture. Or it may mean finding new ways to do so. 'The task,' writes theologian Walter Brueggemann, 'is to empower people to engage in history . . . evoking cries that expect answers, learning to address them where they will be taken seriously, and ceasing to look to the numbed and dull empire that never intended to answer in the first place.'[11]

5.23 People's development within local faith communities can be significant in building their capacity to operate on a wider stage. Congregations of all faiths have been places where people have developed personal confidence, skills, qualities and awareness which has equipped them to operate beyond their 'base'. There can be significant development from involvement in worship itself. However, the practice of deliberative democratic participation – dealing with disagreement without rowing, 'withdrawing', leaving or splitting – may require capacities that need to be explicitly developed.

5.24 The processes of democracy can be particularly perplexing for members of faith communities where authority is located not only (or even mainly) in the popular will but also in prophet, priest, tradition and Scripture. Observing the 'democratic deficit' in many churches, one person told the Commission: 'I think something that holds churches back is an atmosphere of "niceness" and politeness – the feeling that, because we are all Christians, we all have to get on in a happy kind of way. Whereas, sometimes, the situation demands a kind of seriousness that's not really compatible with what is being "polite".'

Developing local democracy within faith communities [B5.4

The Sheffield 'parish development consultations' draw on a growing Anglo-American literature on 'congregational studies' which are partly prompted by the decline and growing dissension within predominantly white Christian churches.[12] Subjecting the familiarity of one's worship community to this perspective can be unsettling, making relative a world that has been experienced as something as natural as the weather. Or it can permit positive sentiments, deep frustrations or 'dull aches' to be explored in a helpfully detached way as a basis for productive and enriching action.

A Commission member observed two consultation workshops, each attended by around 20 members of a Sheffield church on consecutive Saturday mornings in April 2005. The facilitator explained that a basic aim of the sessions was 'to help you "learn to learn", not as individuals but as a body, a congregation'. This aim was addressed by activities that encouraged participants to discover their own unique parish 'wisdom'; that is, 'the way we do things here'. This 'wisdom' was explored by activities that involved.

- *Assembling and reflecting on a 'parish story', using the differing experiences of longstanding and newer members.*
- *Exploring the consequences of congregation size on organization, authority structures and the scope of mission.*
- *Identifying the present main purposes of the church and those that participants would like to prioritize in the future.*
- *Assessing the nature and the extent of a shared church 'outlook' among participants.*

The Sheffield church, slowly growing in membership, needs to address how it moves from a medium-sized to a large congregation. The role and skills required of the vicar may need to change as part of a wider process of organizational change. Or, in identifying the different preferred future purposes of the church, possibilities of both opportunity and conflict come into clearer focus. Is there a shared outlook or are there divergent outlooks? The intended outcome of the sessions was to prompt a shared ongoing revision of the 'parish wisdom' which incorporates and works with this new awareness. 'We can offend other people by doing things that, to us, seem entirely rational,' explained the facilitator. 'The irritation is the result of our mutuality. No one way is right. It is the result of our coming together . . . The maturity of a congregation is seen in the recognition of this mutuality and responding to it positively.'

But he also noted that there can often be a 'culture of evasion', not least in the Church of England, that needs to be countered by the ability to be assertive and 'straightforward'. These are skills that need to be fostered, practised and supported through training in assertiveness and decision-making. The Diocese offers these for churches that request them.

5.25   Local urban congregations need particular support and strategies in building alliances across faiths, for the logic of working together on issues of public concern and in the public arena is a powerful one. For many years, multi-faith forums and networks for dialogue have been established in our big cities and our most ethnically diverse towns. The ground is well prepared to go the next step of taking action together to address shared problems. Working across denominations or faiths gives power to people and their local congregations. The powerlessness of people and marginalized communities which *Faith in the City* diagnosed 20 years ago remains a central problem. Practical strategies for generating the power to act among people of goodwill remain a central challenge, but one which we have seen being met in a number of urban areas. There is huge potential to extend good practice into other places.

A gated world: the search for security

5.26   Alongside gentrification we observe a drive for security and order in our cities. An increased use of surveillance and a rising sense of control over public and private spaces has led to the 'citadalization' of our cities.[14] Physical threat and danger in the form of crime, drugs and terrorism are perceived as predominantly urban problems. They are also realities which have a significant global dimension. The anxiety and suspicion which people feel rarely matches the reality of risk. Nevertheless, that anxiety is real enough – and security has become a key sector in the urban economy, offering a precarious 'peace of mind' to those who are willing and able to pay. Fear brings the opportunity for profit.

5.27   The terrorist attacks in London and New York exacerbated a culture of fear and suspicion of the stranger, but they did not create it. Distrust of strangers is correlated with economic inequality. Both London and New York are places of widening wealth and poverty, where ethnic, racial and religious differences are proxies for economic status. It is not only terrorists who cause divisions to emerge but those who take advantage of the situation – from politicians and religious preachers to those who profit from making our cities citadels of security. One central London church, reflecting on these issues, called upon the story of David and Goliath. David's strength lay in his refusal to depend on the armour of Saul but rather to use the skills and knowledge he had acquired outside the arena of war.

5.28   For a long period, people in Britain had feared a terrorist attack like the one which claimed 52 lives in London on 7 July 2005. For Muslims in Britain, anxiety was heightened by the prospect of rising Islamophobia in the general public were such an attack to occur. In the event, while there was an increase in attacks on Muslims after 7/7, the worst fears of the community have not been realized. This is testament to the good work in building relationships by leaders inside and outside the Muslim community, by inter-faith networks and some public agencies.

5.29   Despite this, many British Muslims fear that 'anti-terror' legislation passed in 2005 gives statutory agencies unjustified and unreasonable powers of intrusion into mosques. The impact of this legislation on community life and on relations between British Muslims and the Government remains to be tested, but such institutionalization of suspicion may well add to levels of mutual mistrust that already run high.

Faith communities and public services

5.30   The many hours committed by people of faith in their communities has, rightly, been recognized by government far more in recent years. The Prime Minister has been effusive, and ministers and policy makers see in faith communities many attributes they would like to nurture in our public services. Indeed, a general invitation has been extended to faith communities to become involved in their delivery.

5.31   The use of faith-based organizations in public service delivery is a controversial issue. There have been some well-organized efforts to promote it;[15] and some vocal opposition, often from secularists who suspect the agenda of faith organizations. Increasingly, critical questions are being posed inside faith communities themselves by people who argue for a 'recovery of confidence' in their essential distinctiveness from the secular realms of the state and the market. For many people of faith, taking God out of their work in the community makes no sense, and if that is the price of working with public funds, they would rather not.

5.32   The toleration of religious faith in publicly funded initiatives has increased in recent years, is in part due to successful lobbying by faith-based initiatives and to the changing attitudes of public officials towards faith. In our view this does not entirely remove the difficulties and risks involved in taking public funds. Even where faith-based organizations are given greater freedom, in principle, to operate by their own values, in practice this can become unwittingly compromised as the powerful culture and demands of statutory bodies seep into previously independent institutions. A further danger is that 'the dominance of the market model in the provision of welfare services, and the demand of competitive tendering for government contracts, frames relations between local faith designated groups in terms of rivalry rather than co-operation'.[17]

5.33   One criticism of the current trend of funding faith-based institutions to deliver public sector objectives is that money is by no means always the most effective guarantor of change. The currency which best enables faith congregations to seek and create change in their localities may not be public money, but the development of independent networks of trust and co-operation worked on patiently at the local level by neighbouring institutions.

The blurring of public and private

5.34   A widely debated trend observed in British cities currently is the increased blurring of public and private sectors. We see this not only where private companies deliver public services but where roles previously held by planning authorities are now handled by developers and other private companies. In many urban 'opportunity areas' including King's Cross in London, private consultation companies are paid to be the 'listening' interface with the local community on proposed redevelopment. Local councillors, sometimes overwhelmed by the scale and complexity of developments, are contracting out their role as political interface with their electorate. This raises questions, not just about the independence of politicians, but about who really benefits from local development and public service reform, and which sections of the population risk losing out.

5.35   It is not our role to reflect in detail on the relationship between public and private, but urban congregations have a clear interest in how public service reform affects people in urban areas, in particular on those most dependent on public services – often the poorest. For public service reform to deliver widespread benefit, including to the most vulnerable, a strong, independent and morally literate citizenry and civil society sector is needed. Such a 'thriving

The cost of wealth

'The horror of being vulnerable to terrorist violence might open our eyes to the vulnerability that in fact underlies the whole globalization process. It is harder to believe that our world is one in which the increase of wealth for a minority can be indefinitely projected without cost. Already the existence of wealthy residential developments surrounded by all the technological refinements of security in many of our cities tells us that the spiral of wealth is also the spiral of threat.'
Archbishop Rowan Williams [16]

public realm'[18] must be distinct from the state and the market. Our concern is that current public sector reform – driven forward energetically by central government, with the vocal support of the business community[19] – comes at a time when we have a historically weak civil society sector and historically low levels of trust in politicians and political institutions.

Civil renewal and democratic deficit

5.36   Neighbourhood renewal programmes and reforms of public services are often described by Government ministers in the language of civil renewal. And our Commission endorses the many positive effects of public spending in deprived urban areas, many of which are associated with neighbourhood renewal programmes. At the same time we have come across widespread disillusionment with the Government's pledge of civil renewal among people from congregations and church organizations who, in good faith, had engaged with statutory bodies and municipal authorities. Many people have expressed real anger to us. They believe that the promise at the heart of civil renewal – of citizens having influence and some power in the governance of their neighbourhoods and cities – has been broken.

5.37   In Birmingham, people with many years' experience in urban regeneration talked of the huge frustration at having 'the goal posts moved repeatedly'.[21] They felt let down, and that they had wasted their time, almost always time given for free. Very often what is open to be discussed and changed has turned out to be limited and ultimately worth little to people who have given time to pursue change for the benefit of their community.

5.38   Writing about the experience of engaging with North Peckham's Single Regeneration Budget programme, a local Baptist minister writes:

> Here was a major redevelopment, tackling difficulties in the build environment ... with many local organizations being asked to respond to plans. It was not dialogue; it was responding. Any attempts to question some of the bases of the plan were lost in the system of council meetings. These included creating employment, a pressing local problem. We were given mixed messages about that, and the outcome was that no permanent jobs were created. The plan meant a 20% reduction in housing provision at a time of growing demand for social housing. This also was challenged but never addressed.' He concludes, 'What central government and local government were not asking for, was any contribution by the local churches which would make any inroads into the political assumptions of those holding the power.'[22]

5.39   Consultation with local people is not only a mantra of public-service managers, it is often actually a condition of receiving funds from central government to regenerate deprived areas. If the instincts in imposing these conditions are laudable, in practice conflicting agendas and instructions from the centre (typically to slim spending but also to listen to the interests of local people) cause real problems. A top-down imperative to 'listen' to local communities can lead to cynicism on the part of public servants, and to disillusion among community leaders, service users and citizens. The Commission found this sort of damaging cynicism and disillusion in diverse areas of urban areas of Britain.

5.40   The gap between the rhetoric and the reality of civil renewal is in danger of driving local congregations either to withdraw completely from public life, or to become drained and co-opted by the shifting agendas of statutory agencies. What is needed are ways for faith communities to make a distinctive and effective contribution to the public life of urban areas. This contribution needs to be both authentic to their primary mission and ministry, and able to deliver real improvements to people's lives. Faith communities have something genuine to offer because members and leaders of urban congregations speak with real authority about the problems of urban Britain. Their churches, mosques and temples are full of people who struggle with those problems every day. These everyday stories of struggle are an invitation to congregations and their faith leaders to consider their public role and voice.

5.41   But if there is widespread mistrust and cynicism about mainstream politics, there is also evidence of a willingness to take part in public life - providing people feel they have the power to frame the terms on which they participate. In 2004, over 1,700 people from different ethnic and religious backgrounds assembled at Methodist Central Hall to present their 'Citizens Agenda for London' to the mayoral candidates. Most were from London's poorest boroughs and communities, people normally dismissed as politically apathetic. People need ways of engaging more fully than by simply protesting from the outside, or being used as volunteers to put sticking plasters on the cracks of society without asking questions of the drive for status, power and profit.

5.42   For members of the Christian communities, prophetic presence and participation in these struggles is the critical core of our urban mission. As Archbishop Rowan Williams puts it, 'The Church exists to connect people at the level of their hunger for a new world . . . this is how the Church makes neighbours - not so much by struggling to find ideas that unite us, not even by struggling to make us like each other, but by giving us a role to play, the role of people all equally eager to be fed by one life-giving food.'[24]

6 A Good City:

Urban Regeneration with People in Mind

Cities in theological perspective

6.1 At the heart of our work as Commissioners is the fundamental question: 'What makes a *good* city?' From Newcastle to Plymouth, we have tried to stimulate a debate around this theme across the country that has involved both Church and secular agencies. And as we have sought to define a values-driven approach to urban regeneration, rooted in our faith, a large part of our task has been trying to discern what these values might be, and how they might embody the Christian vision.

6.2 Where might this vision come from? In Scripture and tradition the city appears as a place of encounter between people and God. It seems that 'the city' often appears as the space between what is and what is to come. It is a place of waiting but also the space in which humanity is called to work for God's purposes. Here are some examples:

- 'Seek the peace and prosperity of the city to which I have carried you into exile. Pray to the Lord for it, because if it prospers, you too will prosper' (Jeremiah 29.7). Even in exile and dislocation, it is possible to make common cause and see something of the good in an alien place.
- The vision of the heavenly city of the book of Revelation (conceived by a church in persecution) is one of suffering but also of ultimate promise.
- Augustine, in his great work *City of God,* sees two cities: the 'heavenly city' and the 'earthly city'. Christians are called to live between the two, attempting to embody a vision of the ultimate and transcendent amid the immanent. The city is a human space, riven with contradictions, but undeniably the place of divine deliverance and covenant.

6.3 Perhaps cities serve as refractions of our deepest understandings of what it means to be human – values and meanings embedded in the physical design of the urban environment. Yet this notion of a city tests the way both Judaism and Christianity understand themselves. Take, for example, the story of Exodus in which Israel encounters God through a journey. Israel is often presented as a migrant people. Even the Temple is not like other, pagan, temples of the period. The covenants delivered on Mount Sinai and to King David are not opposed.[2] Christianity inherits this restlessness. How should Christian congregations embody such restlessness in the fixedness of our cities? Wrestling with the inherited values and assumptions of our cities must remain part of the task of urban faith communities.

6.4 Successive civilizations often embodied in their cities particular ideals and aspirations about the purpose of human society. City life has always reflected the cultures from which it emerged.

6.5 In Ancient Greece, for example, cities were political entities. As political systems they were by no means perfect – since women, slaves and foreigners were all excluded from the rights and responsibilities of citizenship – but it was the concept of urban citizenship and democratic government that characterized those independent Greek city-states. And it is the political nature of the city – identified under the Greeks with democracy, as rule of the people – that is important today, despite the democratic deficit we now experience in much of our urban life.

6.6 The rise of Roman urban settlements, on the other hand, was founded on military and colonial administration, as their empire spread across the known world. Later, the revival of European medieval civilization from around the eleventh century was often fostered by the founding of cities as centres of commerce, learning, and industry. By the time of the Renaissance, great cities such as Florence came to represent the fruits of humanist culture, with attention to great art and culture as well as economic power.

6.7 The Enlightenment and the democratic revolutions of the mid- to late eighteenth century brought down the divine right of kings and promoted the nascent power of the urban manufacturing classes. In the end it was capitalism and the new industrial order – symbolized by the mills and 'manufactories' of cities such as Manchester – that superseded the medieval city, and ushered in modern society by separating the Church from its social pre-eminence and reducing the market to purely economic functions. The capitalist city created an entirely new urban paradigm. With the Industrial Revolution, we see the emergence of the modern city.

6.8 With this change came a fundamental shift in the priorities of land use – which became increasingly subservient to the needs of the city. The environmental impact of this shift would prove enormous and it has remained a theme and a source of conflict for over 200 years. However, the city has become the dominant environment for humans. The early twentieth century saw a rapid development of urban studies as an academic field exploring the distinctive qualities of the modern industrial city. For them, cities such as Manchester, Chicago and New York were characterized by density of population, migration and mobility (not just regionally but internationally), and by cultural, religious, racial and linguistic pluralism.

6.9 Human relationships in modern cities became characterized less by familiarity than by anonymity. And thus a more anonymous, technological, and functional vision of society grew. For some, this feature was to be celebrated and, in many cases, actually made manifest in the style of the urban environment itself.

6.10 The work of the Swiss architect Le Corbusier in the early twentieth century is seen by many as developing a kind of secular utopia (he actually published a book entitled *The Radiant City*) in which the qualities of symmetry, calculation, science, technical-rational design are elevated.[3] However, there has always been a more nostalgic, pastoral strand, as in the English Garden Cities movement, led by people like Ebenezer Howard and Henrietta Barnett, the pioneers of Welwyn Garden City and Letchworth. Here, urban design reflects an attempt to integrate the head and the heart, to locate the convenience of the city amidst the beauty of the countryside.

6.11 It is worth noting that both these examples of modern urban planning assumed that human community can be engineered – that human behaviour can be shaped by the visions and designs of architects and planners with support from economists, politicians and others. By the middle of the twenty-first century most people in the world will live in urban areas. But what assumptions underpin this understanding of human nature as perfectible – or at least malleable – according to our environment? These have been strong themes in many projects of urban design and regeneration.

6.12 Cities have always been expensive, and environmentally difficult to sustain. And history shows that where these issues have not been resolved cities can become truly fragile environments. Yet there is no obvious, feasible alternative as the human population continues to grow. We are at the stage where cities *have to work*. But tackling these issues is more than just a matter of regulation, appliance of science and clever management. As we have said elsewhere in this report, new values – or at least a re-emergence of forgotten or neglected ones – need to be considered and developed. Such values must reflect human satisfaction and purpose of life rather than the present preoccupation with quantity and economic growth.

6.13   We are not arguing that there are too many people on the planet (sadly a preoccupation of some environmentalists), but that gauging individuals by their material worth is leading to both social and environmental degradation.

Cities as spaces of human meaning and making

6.14   Doreen Massey, an urban geographer, talks about the significance of a sense of belonging, and of the importance of fulfilling everyone's innate human potential. She argues that 'what makes a good city' transcends the immediate and tangible and speaks of the quality of life, the need for nurture and of offering a human face to the city.[4]

6.15   Massey writes autobiographically about growing up in Wythenshawe, a large council housing development (a 'garden city') to the south of Manchester immediately after the Second World War. She interweaves her narrative with other stories and analysis: family history, the history of city planning in Manchester, issues of participation and governance and urban theory. She says that 'places are spaces of social relations' – the physical always serves as a window into less tangible dynamics of human interaction.

6.16   Massey raises questions about the ways in which urban design and the built environment make statements about what it means to be human, and to live as communities. The spaces that the city occupy in our cultural imagination are therefore of crucial significance for the way government, business and faith-based organizations promote regeneration and community development. Implicit in our answers to the question, 'What makes a good city?' are understandings of what it means to be human, what undergirds human equity and flourishing, and what, ultimately, constitutes authentic human destiny.

6.17   The only future for cities is a sustainable future. The theme of restlessness – of journey and migration – can be helpful here. Cities tend to see themselves as monoliths over against 'the country', whereas, in fact, in order to work they rely upon sophisticated networks of distribution and exchange. Cities are re-made every day. Geographer David Harvey argues that cities should be understood as ecosystems,[5] and during the work of our Commission we have increasingly come to think of them as 'organic' entities with porous boundaries.

6.18   Christian communities can demonstrate this organic quality. For example, those with eucharistic traditions – in which the ritual of sharing bread and wine is central – must remember that the Church is not concerned to defend its own physical place but to offer a table of friendship as a gift in any and all places. Christian communities must model the organic nature of the city, an ever-present reminder of the organic nature of place as we make and re-make our cities.[6]

6.19   We must recognize that physical space and the urban environment are windows into deeper issues of human value and purpose. In which case, we might ask:

- What implicit values underpin strategies of regeneration in our major cities today?
- Is there a secular doctrine of salvation at work – in models of participation, even in the design of the built environment?
- What can we learn about 'what makes the good city' from the design and the purpose of the buildings we set at its heart?
- What values are embodied in the design of our urban environment, be it the rational, modernist Platonic geometry of Le Corbusier, the pastoral idyll of Ebenezer Howard or the monumental aspirations of our twenty-first-century secular temples, the out-of-town shopping malls? What does urban design say about what we choose to elevate as our objects of worship, our ultimate visions of what it means to be human?
- Where are the signs of the transcendent in our cities?

- Where are the secular equivalents of the 'heavenly city'?

and above all

- What stories do these built environments tell us about ourselves – about who we want to include and who we want to exclude?

6.20　The theologian Timothy Gorringe argues that posing such questions is precisely what theology should be doing. Theology can highlight the spiritual dimensions of built environment, urban planning and community – not in an other-worldly sense, but by cultivating the sensibilities and values that inform collective decisions. He says, 'The spirituality of a culture expresses itself in, and therefore shapes, ethics, but also art, literature, music, religion, cuisine, and building – the whole of everyday life.'[7]

6.21　For Gorringe, the Church is the place where theological or metaphysical values are 'made flesh'. This takes place through the Church's everyday life as a 'servant community' living out narratives of creation, redemption and reconciliation in ways that are exemplary and prophetic. He argues that the Church is an embodiment of humane values and a significant actor in the urban drama – not just in what it says, but also in the way it lives out in microcosm a vision of the good community, the good city. And – as the community meets to eat bread and drink wine at the invitation of one put on trial in a city and executed outside a city's walls – so the goodness of this creation is affirmed.

6.22　The Church has intellectual resources, also. The Christian doctrine of the incarnation is a powerful metaphor with which to explore the questions of what makes a good city. In the Gospels, Jesus – the human face of God – proclaims liberation, as a herald of God's reign, promising the release of the captive and the oppressed. The idea that, in Christ, God occupies a space in this creation is a mighty affirmation of a doctrine of place. That Jesus' death takes place *outside* a city refers to the theme of power in cities and its potential to exclude. In our own cities, Jesus' question, 'Who is my neighbour?' has a particular resonance. It could provoke a congregation to reflect on its special role in a particular neighbourhood. It stirs up further questions too: is the built environment organized in a way that makes it difficult to recognize our neighbours? Does the governance of cities affirm neighbourliness or separateness?

6.23　The story of creation – of humanity created in the image and likeness of God – is another means of thinking theologically about cities. Cities are products of human fabrication but also expressions of our humanity as creatures before God. We can see the built environment, and the human creativity that it represents, as a kind of 'sacrament' of transcendence – the fruits of human fabrication as a crucial vehicle of divine disclosure. The crucial question is: which values govern what we make? Are these the values of justice, empowerment and solidarity – or inequity, dispossession and fragmentation? Can the inhabitants of a city trust that the city works for the common good?

6.24　Similarly, our beliefs about the Holy Spirit lead us to ask, 'What does it mean to build community together?' The story of Pentecost and the origins of the Church encapsulate, in narrative form, an idea of the Spirit as something that harnesses human difference into a coherent vision of the kingdom – a new common dwelling place for humanity in the image of God. That vision of unity amidst diversity is a powerful story for plural and fragmented cities.

6.25　Diversity and unity are powerfully presented by the fact that major cities are now multi-faith. In other words, there are different sacred spaces, and different understandings of sacred space, within our cities. In Britain, houses have been changed into mosques, becoming in turn prestigious landmarks. The same has happened with Hindu temples and Sikh gurdwaras, as well as 'secular' or non-defined faith sacred places. The ability to respond to these diverse needs for sacred space is an indicator of a city and its residents' well-being. Again, for Christianity, the theme of restlessness is important. Christian communities need places to perform their rituals but don't need to command or control space. Religious communities must not mirror the turf wars between developers, by engaging in battles over sacred space.

Building the 'good city'

6.26   The Delivering Sustainable Communities Summit held in Manchester in 2005 was hosted by the Deputy Prime Minister and supported by senior cabinet members. The largest event of its kind ever held in the UK, it brought together more than 2,000 delegates from public and private sectors, government, and the building and 'regeneration' industries. There was little doubt that the focus was on material regeneration of urban communities and the criteria used to judge successful regeneration was usually economic and material. What mattered was the level of economic activity and the appearance of the new communities. Status, power and profit appeared to be far more dominant than issues to do with how people lived and the quality of their living environment. That said, the report back on the Summit[8] produced a useful definition of sustainable communities. Sustainable communities:

- Are places where people want to live and work, now and in the future;
- Meet the diverse needs of existing and future residents, are sensitive to their environment and contribute to a high quality of life. They are safe and inclusive, well planned, built and run, and offer equality of opportunity and good services for all;
- Are diverse, reflecting their local circumstances. There is no standard template to fit them all, but they should be:
    - Active, inclusive and safe
    - Well run
    - Environmentally sensitive
    - Well designed and built
    - Well connected
    - Thriving
    - Well served
    - Fair for everyone.

6.27   In two years of listening and consultation as a Commission, it has become clear that regeneration strategies that do not start with the hopes and expectations of local people's - that is what local people value - are doomed to fail. Any strategy needs to be responsive enough to embrace, rather than simply tolerate, communities' own understanding of and aspirations for their local environment.

6.28   The Government's regeneration and renewal process involves clearly identifying your outcome and your target group, a process which might achieve accountability, but which, in the process, entraps us into reducing people to problems and issues.

6.29   The history of regeneration in Manchester's Moss Side offers a case in point. In research for the William Temple Foundation, residents spoke of the disconnection between the urban regeneration that takes place and the people whose local environment it affects. For some, it is so much investment and effort for little obvious return:

> *Over the past ten years we have seen a lot of money being pumped into the Moss Side area and yet when you look at the black community, young people are more likely to get involved or be over represented in terms of prison population, their underachievement at schools and opportunities seem very much limited. So over the last ten years really Moss Side doesn't seem to have moved on in terms of wealth or jobs.*

6.30   The research highlights widespread distrust and indignation over the way the regeneration industry often 'parachutes in' to a 'deprived' community. Whether led by local authority or private sector professionals, the industry brings with it a set of values that suggests that what has been achieved in the past is bad and the new utopia lies just around the corner. They seem to be saying, 'We have the money to show you how it can be.'

6.31　The part that the physical environment plays in regeneration strategies can exemplify a 'professionals know best' culture, which exists despite the presence of professionals who are motivated by faith and goodwill. Some of the financial investment in Moss Side has been deployed on 'environmental improvements', elements of which, such as better waste disposal, are welcome. But changing the look of a place without reference to the community often sends a signal that the authorities do what they want and know what's best. Such 'improvements' may not look like 'improvements'. As Commissioners, we argue that changes must be achieved through genuine partnership.

6.32　And local churches have genuine contributions to make. One might be by introducing the challenging and unfashionable idea of 'holiness' into the regeneration process. This involves seeing people and their communities in all their complexity and in recognizing that they (we) don't always make rational sense. This is a long-term process which involves giving people full attention and entering a relationship with them.

The ecology of the city

6.33　Justice in our relationship with our environment is vital for the common good. The common good refers us to ecology – to the goods we have in common, to those non-human species with which we share this world. Manchester, for example, seems to be governed by a belief that more development is needed in order to express our humanity. Although new designs and programmes may have environmental factors built in (such as low-energy-use buildings) our demands on the environment continue to increase overall.

6.34　As more people crowd into cities, the quality of our shared existence becomes a big issue. We believe that The United Nations Millennium Statement about values to reduce the degradation of the ecosystem must become central to Government policy on urban regeneration.[9]

Values of regeneration

6.35　As a representative group from the faith communities, we are proposing an alternative values-based approach to regeneration that – if adopted by the regeneration industry – would lead to better cities. It is imperative to begin with people, their well-being, their happiness and the understanding and use of their environment. People in their communities are the bearers of values. In the context of the built environment, Timothy Gorringe commends the Christian values of justice, empowerment, situatedness, and diversity.[10] Such values offer a way of re-considering the theme of people's well-being in the city. Through this approach, it should be possible to develop and creatively use tools based on an identification of needs. From there we can plan (with justice) our urban communities socially, economically and physically.

Core cities

6.36　Whereas we argue that regeneration should be centred in the people and their well-being, the Government's focus remains largely economic. *Our Cities are Back*[11] published by the Office of the Deputy Prime Minister in December 2004, showed how city centres in the eight regional 'core cities' (Birmingham, Bristol, Leeds, Liverpool, Manchester, Newcastle, Nottingham and Sheffield) have been transformed in recent years by jobs and investment. The report set out steps for building on this success – through exploiting the economic strength of the core cities to create more prosperous regions and sustainable communities.

Its key recommendation is that neighbouring cities need to work more closely together in their 'city region', to increase their economic competitiveness and accelerate growth. The report's specific action plans to improve city competitiveness include work to further develop transport planning, improve local knowledge and skills, and build closer economic linkages between London and the core cities.

Mapping the 'good city'

6.37 If we compare these views with those from two of the actual core cities we see how far removed government is from local people. Prior to the Government's announcement of its 'sustainable communities' definition, Sheffield City Council proposed the following '10 Features of a Successful City' that might be taken as indicators of a city's well-being:
- A strong economy
- A well-educated workforce
- A vibrant city centre
- Attractive successful neighbourhoods – cities need to provide for a wide range of lifestyles, so we need a variety of neighbourhoods that offer distinctive facilities that reflect the aspirations of the people who live there
- A healthy population, low crime
- Good transport systems
- Good cultural and sporting facilities
- Cosmopolitan and inclusive
- Well run, sustainable and well regarded – well governed, playing a responsible role in terms of its environmental impact and a place that others want to visit or do business

6.38 As part of the Commission's consultation, the Diocese of Newcastle held 'Urban Hearings' in 2004 and found that a good city:
- Values its inhabitants
- Is diverse and inclusive
- Is a well-led city
- Has an active civil society
- Is always changing
- Attracts the wealth-creators
- Shares its wealth
- Is a learning city
- Has opportunities for all
- 'A good city is big enough to allow anonymity, a strong fiscal base, provide employment of the required nature, have an artistic and cultural life, have a robust local governance, and can compete with other cities to attract investment in all resources. At the same time the city has to be small enough to be understood on a human scale and allow human dignity, to ensure that consumers maintain a link with producers, to allow family and social networks to thrive so that people can know and be known, to enable peer influence to exert a beneficial restraint on behaviour.'

- Or, as one young person involved in the consultation process stated: 'In short, a good city is one in which people do not merely exist or survive but *live*.'

6.39 The convergence between the Sheffield and Newcastle documents is remarkable. We believe that such a person-centred and creation-minded, value-driven approach to urban regeneration must now impact upon government policy. However monumental its buildings, or successful its economy, *people* are always the heart of a city. In fact, the two have often grown together – and a sense of place needs to be understood as much in terms of social and even spiritual value as its economic value. Place is always more than simply economic space. Indeed, as the geographer David Harvey points out, some communities will cling to their traditional place even to their economic detriment.[12] This means that to a specific community place is more than environment alone. History or memory is also a vital constituent of place. We cannot think of place without reference to a people, its environment, and its memory.[13] Where there is a divorce between these attributes of place we often witness a general drain on the natural resources of a city. Where a city is closely associated with a striking and valued topographical feature or even cultural attribute this can, paradoxically, be degraded because of the separation of economic well-being from social and environmental well-being.

Who is the good city for?

6.40   People living in poverty often fall foul of regeneration and gentrification. They find themselves at the wrong end of the growing gap between rich and poor, and unable to remain in redeveloped communities. They can literally find themselves outside gated developments where the better off are seen to be protecting themselves from the poor. The fact that the poor are much more likely to be victims of crime is ignored.

6.41   Also, problems of racism remain within our urban areas. The Stephen Lawrence report has not cured institutional racism within police forces or local neighbourhoods. The racist murder of the black teenager Anthony Walker in Liverpool signals how serious the problems remain.

6.42   Politicians are beginning to recognize the importance of old-fashioned virtues of selflessness and common decency in the cause of moderating people's behaviour, encouraging self-discipline and an awareness of the needs of others. This is the agenda that underpins the current emphasis on countering antisocial behaviour. Frank Field observes that 'The distinguishing mark of anti-social behaviour is that each single instance does not by itself warrant a counter legal challenge. It is in its *regularity* that antisocial behaviour wields its destructive force. It is from the repetitive nature of the nuisance that antisocial behaviour is born.'[14]

6.43   Governmental encouragement of local authorities to make use of antisocial behaviour orders (ASBOs) is an attempt to re-balance justice towards the innocent. But it is questionable whether it is feasible or desirable for government to legislate with a view to changing people's behaviour for the better. Law and politics cannot make people good. The risk is that, by using legislation to try and curtail antisocial behaviour, the Government is exposed as not having the power or capacity to deliver on its policies.

6.44   Beyond doubt, heeding the day-to-day needs of others has its roots in the values and practices of the Christian teaching that has dominated our history. We are inheritors of the social capital that grew out of past Christian belief. However, Christianity is unlikely to again play the role it once did in developing public ideology. Nevertheless, a peaceable city and peaceable society needs people who are willing to think both beyond themselves and beyond immediate gratification.

6.45   The other cause of antisocial behaviour which comes under the spotlight is families failing to pass on to their children the respectfulness and civility, that are essential to civilized living. But focusing on the faltering nature of institutional religion and inadequate parenting can serve to distract us from the impact of market drivers that turn the immediate fulfilment of ones longings into a virtue. It is a salient fact that market capitalism goes into decline if the market is populated by people who exercise self-restraint, are aware of the needs of others and reflect on the well-being of the planet. The market economy has brought unimagined benefits to the lifestyle of many in the western world but there is growing awareness of a downside – that the best kind of consumers for a growing economy are those whose perspective is limited to their own needs.

Pastors take to the streets

A bold new initiative from the churches made its debut on the streets of Lewisham in south London: 'street pastors', as they are known, are part of an anti-crime initiative after closing time. The Revd Les Isaac of Ascension Trust developed the project after visiting churches in Jamaica and reflecting on how the UK church could be active in tackling urban problems. Street pastors are concerned members of local churches who are prepared to undergo a 12-day training course and to commit to one Friday or Saturday night a month (10 p.m. – 4 a.m.) visiting pubs, clubs and night-time venues to engage and care for the marginalized and socially excluded – particularly young people. The scheme has been extended and Street Pastors have been operating successfully in Birmingham, Manchester, Leicester and other parts of London.[15]

[B6.1]

6.46   A range of complex issues must be negotiated if our behaviour as citizens is to add to the common good and if economic well-being is to be sustainable. Such concerns are already at the heart of the local regeneration and renewal initiatives shaping many parts of our cities, particularly areas that experience multiple deprivation.

6.47   As the need for greater social cohesion has become a priority of government policy, there have been signs that a shared values-driven approach to regeneration, around which neighbourhoods can gather, is also becoming a priority, particularly in areas of mixed faith and ethnic population. This must be encouraged as we focus on the cities that we wish to create for the twenty-first century.

6.48   In the Newcastle Good City Debate on valuing its inhabitants, some of the comments included:

- 'Charity is for me a key word. We're not very forgiving or very charitable. I hope that we could have a society where we listen more to each other.'
- 'A good city values its young people. The public are more anxious about public disorder than ever before. Adults have lost confidence in relating to young people. There is also a loss of "significant" adults for young people.'
- 'Newcastle is a Cinderella city. There are a whole host of people who do not access the centre, the exciting bits, and the wealthy bits.'
- 'A good city is caring and compassionate – for example, how well do we look after carers?'

6.49   Richard Rogers' Urban Task Force recently reviewed government progress over six years in *Towards a Strong Urban Renaissance*. [16] The report highlights the need for design excellence, social well-being and environmental responsibility set within a viable and sustainable economic, legislative and delivery framework. It also highlights the structural incoherence besetting the redevelopment of Thames Gateway in London. We welcome the vision that the Task Force has brought but regret that they take such a constrained and limited view of social well-being, compared to their first report. Where is the argument about the values or the soul of the city – themes that make the difference for the best cities in the world?

New visions for the city: international perspectives

6.50   We have been particularly impressed by the work of some urban planners and geographers who are pointing to practical visions of urban design and planning which spring from this value-driven approach. Leonie Sandercock's *Mongrel Cities* [17] offers a radically different approach to urban planning and design than that prevalent in most local authority planning departments – or indeed the Office of the Deputy Prime Minister. In fact, it is sometimes closer to the stuff of the Old Testament prophetic visionary as the quotation with which we opened this chapter demonstrates.

6.51   Urban geographers Ash Amin, Doreen Massey and Nigel Thrift pick up some of these themes in a British context in their book, *Cities for the Many not for the Few*.[18] Here they make the argument that the way we use space in a city will determine the way in which its citizens interact, their quality of life and even their economic performance.

6.52   The Rogers Report is clearly sensitive to these issues, in pressing for a holistic and sustainable urban experience, good quality design and architecture, compact sites, and pleasant open spaces. We welcome its acknowledgement of the spatiality of the city. But this spatiality is also about dealing with the effects of diverse communities and interests living together in close proximity. This is why we have stressed the rights of being, becoming and interconnecting in the city – rights which do not flow by themselves from the ways in which physical space is organized, but also from the developmental and expressive opportunities given to people.

6.53   Two of our Commission members spent time looking critically at the city of Chicago to reflect on how it has tackled some of the issues we have outlined above. Chicago is a global city with a richly diverse population, as destination for migrants for two centuries. But its planners and leaders are also aware that continuing economic success depends on relocating it in international markets such as information technology, finance, heritage, and tourism rather than manufacturing. In this, Chicago mirrors the experience of many UK cities. Its urban revival has been built on making the city more attractive to a new generation of incomers: the professional middle classes, new commercial ventures and business or holiday visitors.

6.54   Yet for some the process of gentrification has come at a price: as rising property values – associated with the influx of professional classes and rising commercial rents – have resulted in less affordable accommodation for those on low wages or benefits. Chicago, with its reputation for being a city of neighbourhoods, is finding that the multi-ethnic character of these neighbourhoods is being destroyed as some ethnic groups are being driven to the edge of the city by economic pressures. Those in low-wage service sector jobs in the city centre find themselves travelling over an hour into the city centre – with serious consequences for family life and greater financial cost to the employee. Belatedly, Mayor Daley's City Authority has begun to look for a quota of social housing within every new development.

6.55   There are lessons here for all English cities. Until Urban Splash's involvement with the redevelopment of New Islington in Manchester, the city's regeneration strategy offered little thought to socially mixed developments. There is considerable evidence that the regeneration of large parts of central Manchester and Salford has been accompanied by the continued decline of the 'excluded' areas. Energy goes into physical regeneration of city centres in the first instance without regard to the social consequences.

6.56   But it is not only people on low wages or benefits who are excluded from living in some cities. Those on average incomes are also excluded, including hundreds of thousands of public sector workers vital to the well-being of the city. The situation in London is the most perverse example of a growing crisis in a number of property hotspots across the country. Key workers are faced with several undesirable options. They can rent privately at unsustainable levels, share housing, commute long distances to work, or switch to a more lucrative profession. There is growing evidence that housing problems are a major factor in recruitment crises in both education and the health service. It is no coincidence that the areas where teacher shortages are most acute correlate strongly with areas where house prices are highest.

6.57   Campaigners have forced housing back onto the political agenda and the Government has responded by introducing Key Worker Living schemes such as shared ownership and subsidized rentals. Those eligible for assistance include social workers, fire fighters, and prison and probation service staff, in addition to teachers and nurses. The Government is also turning to the planning system to ensure that more affordable housing is provided on new private developments.

6.58   We have serious doubts as to whether any values, other than the profit, motive undergird the introduction of casinos and extended licensing hours into our city centres. The shocking level of personal debt that already exists in our society raises serious issues about the long-term health of an economy built on the sand of so much personal indebtedness. The Methodist Church and the Salvation Army are not alone in pointing out that the casino culture only adds to the social problems of a city – while the meagre economic gain is in low-wage employment as the bulk of the profits are exported out of the cities.[19] Similarly, public spaces in cities are threatened and not enhanced by the encouragement of an environment conducive to binge drinking and public drunkenness which is interpreted by the drinks industry as 'lively night life'.

6.59   We were impressed by the way in which public space has been developed in Chicago. The most attractive lakeside has been preserved for public access, creating safe recreational space for young and old. The millennium park right at the heart of the city combines an open-air concert hall and a fountain sculpture, 'Gargoyles for the Millennium', which provides laughter and fun for children and adults. It is free; it speaks of diversity and inclusiveness and is a wonderful meeting place. Next to it is a sculpture by Anish Kapoor designed to reflect the park and the urban skyline in its stainless-steel surface, producing a hall of mirrors effect in which visitors see themselves reflected against the city panorama. This encourages everyone to take an active interest in their surroundings, to appreciate their unmistakably urban environment and to locate themselves within the living heart of the city.

6.60 These are examples of the sort of planning and architecture that Leonie Sandercock and Doreen Massey are urging us to take seriously. They inspire us with how urban design and the provision of public space might create a positive, accessible environment for citizens.

6.61 While some UK cities, such as Manchester and Birmingham have begun to provide city centre spaces which have some of these qualities, in the main we continue to allow developers to grab the best of land close to water. A trip down the Thames from the Tower of London to the Thames Barrier and beyond illustrates how little of regenerated Docklands riverside has been left for public space: where there is public space, it appears neither to have received adequate investment nor to have been designed to serve the needs of new local communities. It seems to bear witness to a model of regeneration in which the powerful forces of commerce sideline the needs of local people if they do not generate economic returns.

6.62 The attraction of building by water has meant that land close to canal banks, urban rivers like the Irwell between Manchester and Salford and the Aire in Leeds are not seen as potentially attractive public open space but as a development opportunity. We have something to learn from our European neighbours and cities like San Antonio, Texas about a proper balance between commercial pressures and the creation of good cities, which provide spaces that lift the human spirit.

6.63 The Director of Planning in the City of Vancouver, which has engaged in highly successful urban regeneration, is quoted by Leonie Sandercock as offering a model of an approach to planning which we believe needs to be heard by the Office of the Deputy Prime Minister and local planning authorities in this country:

> We have an unusual attitude about development here. Our attitude is, if you don't measure up, we're not afraid to say No in this city. Many cities are so afraid to say 'No' to a developer and so they get what they deserve. But for those cities it may be above all important to promote business growth. We want quality of life first . . .

> We have an ability to create a city that is to some degree contrary to globalization, contrary to the homogenization of cities going on around the world. It is very unique, and it is very interesting that it actually competes with those world cities not by trying to be what they are but by being an alternative that they can never be. This comes down to the quality of life in the city. [20]

6.64 Vancouver is one of the most successful cities in the world in providing quality of life for its citizens. It has not pursued urban regeneration at any cost but a balanced development making a judgement that the economic success of a development can follow on from a values-based approach to planning.

6.65 When it comes to the imminent Thames Gateway development in London, the Commission recommends a radically different approach to waterside development than we have witnessed in London's Docklands. We would like to believe that this enormous opportunity will carry some of the hallmarks of creative city planning we identified in Vancouver but we remain pessimistic, a sense confirmed by Richard Rogers' own critique of the incoherent approach to this area. This is a development in which too many interested parties are

producing incoherence as developers again lead the regeneration. A targeted number of new homes is not a cornerstone on which to build a good environment in which people want to live.

6.66 Some of our members visited Poundbury in search of lessons that might transfer to urban social design. In 1987, West Dorset District Council selected Duchy land to the west of Dorchester for future expansion of the town. The Prince of Wales took the opportunity to work with the council to contribute a pioneering urban addition to this ancient market town. The architect and urban planner, Leon Krier, prepared the overall development concept with the aim of creating an autonomous new extension within the context of traditional Dorset architecture. Priority in Poundbury was given to people, rather than cars, with the emphasis on building a thriving sense of community, and where the positioning of buildings is determined by the topography of the site rather than the highway engineer.

6.67 This year (2006) work begins on a similar scheme adapted for an urban context. A unique scheme, led by Contingley Cornerstone Centre and St Michael and All Angels Church, Cottingley partnering with the local Council, aims to regenerate the centre of this urban estate in Bradford. A new centre will provide wide-ranging community facilities including a hall, a new church, IT room, GP surgery, pre-school nursery, elderly day-care facility, youth room, respite care for young disabled people and arts and crafts room. A housing element will provide 52 affordable homes for purchase. It is regeneration from the bottom up. The people who will use and benefit from the £8.5 million scheme are the ones who have made it happen.

6.68 'The interest and commitment of the Prince of Wales has been a significant factor,' explained the Revd Suzanne Pinnington. 'Combined with local leadership and the desire of community to build a new sense of community, this has made this ambitious project a reality. The Cottingley Cornerstone Centre is a beacon of hope for the future and it is hoped that it will be seen a model of good practice for other community development initiatives nationwide.'[22]

6.69 There is still a dearth of exciting, risky architecture in our regenerated cities, in comparison with the quality of design in cities like Vancouver, Chicago, and Barcelona. The one-off flagship project does not compensate for a plethora of dull flats and office blocks or the unimaginative space which is the urban shopping centre.

6.70 We have no doubt that the stated government policies towards regeneration – with their emphasis on the quality of life and sustainability of new urban communities – are welcome. We have tried to show what we believe contributes to the good city and where there is still a considerable gap between intent and practice. While there has been progress in tackling poverty, we believe a huge challenge lies ahead if the good city is to fulfil its promise of well-being for its citizens. This will require a radical shift from government at both local and national levels, in how we approach regeneration – an approach which allows those who will actually live in these cities to play the lead role in design and development. Builders and developers must respond to their needs.

6.71 All of this means, that government – as part of its assessment of the outcomes of urban regeneration projects – must measure improvements in the local ecosystem. It must also, as a priority, measure well-being and happiness.

6.72 Urban-based faith communities will be important stakeholders within these discussions, their support and participation as partners is critical in the successful emergence of the good city. Alongside this, the churches must lead a debate with other faith communities about the provision of sacred space within our communities, not least in looking for space which could be held and used in common by all.

7.1 At the heart of a 'good city', there needs to be 'good people'. We are not talking – as we said in Chapter 4 – about being 'nice', we mean people who are prepared to look beyond themselves and their own needs. To reiterate what we said in Chapter 5, underlying what it means to make a good city is an understanding of what it means to be human.

7.2 The major dividend of faithful capital is people motivated by a moral sense that other people and their circumstances matter. There is a duty and purpose-driven enthusiasm for regeneration and transformation – and not simply in some mystical or spiritualized sense. Often this bears fruit in partnerships across what would commonly be regarded as divides – 'bridging' or 'linking' is how we described it in Chapter 3. This is good news for urban areas.

7.3 It must be said that churches are sometimes introverted and pietistic – not always aware of what is happening to the communities in which they are set. They are not always aware of the policies created by local and national government for the regeneration of those communities. But by no means all, or even most churches, or other faith communities, are like that.

7.4 Because of their understanding of the Bible, many feel an imperative to throw in their lot with whoever is committed to regeneration. This commitment leads them to being involved with many agencies, including both local and national government. They also feel called to analyse, understand and critique the structures, policies and programmes they encounter. They try to discern when their involvement with such programmes is in conflict with their own agenda for mission.

7.5 So, why are faith communities that are involved in partnerships concerned with urban regeneration?

Vision for Newham

'I chair a group of evangelical charismatic Christians . . . our vision is that God's kingdom would come in Newham, that we would see truth and justice, that people would be treated equally and rightly, so we share those aspirations and goals with the Council.'

Baptist Minister, Newham

A Christian view

7.6 Regeneration is a familiar concept to people of faith. It is about making a fresh start, becoming transformed, being 'born again'. Although this is often interpreted in an individualistic way, nevertheless, within the Judeo-Christian tradition it is essentially communal.

7.7 There is a theme which runs from the beginning to the end of the Bible – God's created world is spoiled by the selfish activity of men and women, but the promise of God is that restoration is possible. Looking back to the beginning, perfection is embodied in a garden; looking forward to the end, perfection is seen as a city.

7.8 The longing for such a 'New Jerusalem' is buried deep within the Christian consciousness and reinforced every time we say the Lord's Prayer, 'thy kingdom come on earth as it is in heaven'.

7.9 There is a covenant relationship between God and creation, and its acceptance is spelled out (Exodus 24.3–8) when the Hebrew people made an altar and threw over it the blood of animals they had killed. The terms of the covenant were read out and the people accepted them. 'Then he took the book of the covenant, and read it in the hearing of the people, and they said, "All that the Lord has spoken we do, and we will be obedient".' The blood of the same animals was thrown over the people binding God and people together by blood.

7.10 That act was the culmination of their desert wanderings. They had been slaves in Egypt and now they were heading for the land promised to them. But what sort of society would it be? What would it look like? Would it be like Egypt – a Pharaoh at the top of the social pyramid, slaves at the bottom – or would it be different? Throughout the rest of the Hebrew Scriptures there is a constant refrain, 'It shall not be for you as it was in Egypt'. They were going to create a quite different kind of society.

7.11   They would not leave elderly and slow moving parents to die in the desert. They would honour father and mother, carrying them if need be. And in their dotage their children would carry them in turn and they would live long in the land which the Lord God would give them.

7.12   After the incident with manna in the wilderness, where the food the Israelites hoarded went bad (Exodus 16), they would never take more food than they needed for the day, otherwise it would become corrupted and would corrupt them. They would never take all the crops for themselves they would leave some for 'the widow, the fatherless and the stranger'.

7.13   Conscious that each family would be given the privilege and responsibility of caring for part of the land, they realized that it would not be long before some had huge tracts of land and some had none. In response they created 'The year of Jubilee'. Every 50 years they would start again. Land that had been bought or taken would be given back. Within the Covenant they would create a different society. It would not be for them as it had been in Egypt.

7.14   But, of course, it didn't happen like that. As far as we know the Year of Jubilee was never implemented. Institutional religion was substituted for the radical demands of justice and it was this that provoked the ire of the prophets: 'I hate, I despise your festivals, I take no delight in your solemn assemblies . . . but let justice roll down like waters and righteousness like an ever-flowing stream' (Amos 5.21–24). One prophet, Jeremiah, realized that although the people had neglected the covenant, God had not. He foresaw a day when there would be a new covenant.

7.15   The night before Jesus was crucified he gave the disciples the cup of wine and said, 'This is the new covenant in my blood.' This time there was no altar, but a cross; no animals killed, but Jesus, and it is his teaching which make up he terms of this new covenant. He asked the lawyer, '"What is written in the law? What do you read there?" He answered, "You shall love the Lord your God with all your heart, and with all your soul, and with all your strength, and with all your mind, and your neighbour as yourself." And he said to him, "you have given the right answer, do this and you will live"' (Luke 10.26–28). 'I was hungry and you gave me food, I was thirsty and you gave me something to drink. I was a stranger and you welcomed me. I was naked and you gave me clothing, I was sick and you took care of me, I was in prison and you visited me . . . Truly I tell you, just as you did it to one of the least of these, you did it to me' (Matthew 25.35–40). When Christians share that meal they commit themselves to that covenant and its demands of justice and mercy.

7.16   Informed with this biblical understanding, Christians believe that things can and should be different. We have the ongoing task of translating the will of this transcendent God into the realities of day-to-day politics. We are therefore called to analyse, understand and critique the structures, policies and programmes we encounter. Our struggle for God's reign involves acting as advocates for those whose voice is rarely heard, and empowering the excluded. We are compelled to stand alongside them and to form alliances with them and with others who work for the same purposes.

Values shared with other faiths

7.17   Until comparatively recently the Christian churches have had a virtual monopoly in Britain of faith-based social action and the discussion of the social, economic and political implications of belief. At the time of writing government and local authority officials are rushing to improve their understanding of religions and remedy their occasional hostility. In dealing with Muslim and Sikh

Justice for kids
'All that stuff of the kingdom that Jesus was talking about, so where there is the appalling injustice, I mean you can almost see Amos speaking against it . . . you know . . . sod Sheffield First talking about their regeneration strategy, let's have some justice for these kids turning to drugs.'
Baptist Minister, Sheffield

A Catholic view
'In the Catholic Church this has come mainly through papal encyclicals, but then other things kind of tag on with it. It has developed into a rather sophisticated and extensive literature on church social involvement – the involvement of the church in the world, for the good of the world, for the sake of justice, welfare, helping the poor – that sort of thing. So I think that regeneration sits easily with the social teaching of the church.'
Catholic National Officer

communities they have treated them as minority ethnic groups, discouraging overt reference to their faith.

7.18   In a recent piece of fieldwork Greg Smith, of the Centre for Institutional Studies discerned common core values among people of different faiths who were engaged in regeneration and community development:

- Peace and co-operation – people of all faiths and none make the presumption that in an open and democratic society most people are willing to live at peace and strive to co-operate with others.
- Social justice and equality – these are values which seem to be shared across the boundaries of faith.
- Loving your neighbour – this injunction is not the monopoly of the Judeo-Christian tradition. [1]

7.19   Who is my neighbour?' asked the lawyer in the Gospel of Luke. It is a question that requires a new response in every generation and every culture. From an Islamic perspective the neighbour isn't just your next door neighbour – it is 14 houses in all directions. That is the starting point of the neighbourhood, so it extends therefore a sense of community, a sense of belonging. We are talking about citizenship, irrespective of creed, language, race or background.

7.20   The regeneration of our cities is almost always presented in secular and economic terms. But the fact that this concept has theological roots changes the dynamic. The recognition that regeneration is the hope for communities and not simply individuals motivates people of faith, quite naturally, to enter into partnership with each other, government and other agencies.

Partnerships with each other

7.21   Churches form all sorts of partnerships with each other and with other faiths. Many use nationally available organizations as a starting point. For example:

- **Churches Together in Britain and Ireland**, and Churches Together in England, help and encourage churches of all denominations to work more closely together in their work and witness.
- **The Evangelical Alliance** has developed Christian Action Networks across the country. These are a means of linking local churches, projects and individuals who are concerned about community involvement and social action.
- **The Inter Faith Network for the UK** works to build good relations between the different religious communities in the UK at both national and local levels. It works with its member bodies to help make this a country marked by mutual understanding and respect between religions, where all can practise their faith with integrity.
- **Faithworks** works across all denominations offering expertise and advice to churches at local level. It sets up local networks which provide legal entities, accountability, insurance as well as back office support. Supplying this at a network level leaves the local church to follow its passion.
- At the time of writing, **The Christian-Muslim Forum** launched in January 2006, is an initiative to help Muslims and Christians to live in harmony, and is the product of several years' work. The 20-strong Forum is guided by eight presidents, four from each faith. It is chaired by the Bishop of Bolton, the Rt Revd David Gillett, and the vice-chairman is Dr Ataullah Siddiqui from the Islamic Foundation in Leicester.
- **The Church Urban Fund** (CUF) set up as a key recommendation of *Faith in the City*, has done more than any other organization to enable churches and other faith organizations to enter into partnerships and projects in areas too deprived for other organizations to risk investing in. The CUF's expertise in making grants to hard-to-reach communities is exceptional. Government policy and practice would benefit from harnessing these skills.

7.22 Churches are involved in many local collaborations, from renting out church halls for parent and toddler groups to entering into partnership arrangements with local businesses for regeneration or neighbourhood renewal. Faith communities, in different partnerships, are playing a major role in the regeneration of our towns and cities. They are often seen as the catalyst or 'honest broker' in bringing together federations of community groups.

Responding to Government initiatives

7.23 The Government, partly in search of social order and partly in order to fill the gap created by limited social welfare provision, is currently seeking partnerships with faith-based organizations. It has also committed itself to a greater religious literacy, demonstrated by the formation of the Home Office's Cohesion and Faiths Unit, and the appointment of a 'faith envoy' for the Prime Minister. Also, the Regional Development Agencies have reserved places for co-opted representatives from the churches and other faith communities. Local authorities now have officers responsible for liaison with faith communities. And in 2004 the Home Office produced a report, *Working Together: Co-operation between Government and Faith Communities*.[2]

7.24 Many faith leaders are embarked on partnerships with government – such as sitting on Local Strategic Partnerships (LSPs), heading up Neighbourhood Renewal or Surestart schemes. But the Church lacks mechanisms to support those involved, so is not in a good position to pool experience and share good practice.

7.25 Because clergy and congregations have local roots, the Church is in a position to recognize the complexity of a neighbourhood's needs. In this, it has the advantage over government, which has a tendency only to see issues. At its best, the Church can offer a sense of wholeness, honesty and truth – offering the kind of 'patient attention', which the Archbishop of Canterbury commends as a feature of faithful capital – that can only be given 'by those closest to the ground'.[3]

7.26 The Diocese of Birmingham, for instance, became one of many partners in the Flourishing Neighbourhoods Project. The then Bishop of Birmingham, Dr John Sentamu, said, 'We became involved in this Project because it concerns issues which are fundamental to the way we live together here in Birmingham, how we use the vast resources we have (compared to the rest of the world), and how we share them.'[4]

7.27 The Commission visited the Project and appreciated the complexities of such a wide body of partners trying to work with the City Council. We were impressed by innovations like reciprocal relationships between a firm of solicitors and community development workers. The firm employed community development workers and one of its lawyers was, in turn, seconded to a Flourishing Neighbourhood team.

7.28 In a different region, Samuel Wells tells the story of the transformation of his parish in Norwich through partnership with the Government's New Deal for Communities. 'The philosophy,' he says, 'is simple – to give deprived communities the opportunity to regenerate themselves.' They do this by offering them support, encouraging them to form partnerships with business and statutory agencies and making funding dependent on evidence of inclusive working and general propriety. And they insist that the key decisions affecting the future of the community are taken in and by the community. 'One might say,' he explains, 'that a difference between the rich and the poor is that the rich suffer from their own mistakes, whereas the poor suffer both from their own mistakes and from the mistakes of the rich.'[5]

7.29 Church and community, he argues, have been transformed by three approaches:
- **Patience:** simply waiting for the time when the small disruptive element in the community grew up, expressed their anger in a different way, or found alternative outlets for their energies.

- **Youth work:** offering young people a mixture of hospitality and constructive projects – including youth clubs, football teams, dance clubs, trips, sleepovers and discos.
- **Recognizing a changing status for the Church:** formerly the Church acted like a failing parent, isolated, surrounded by young people who felt they had no stake in society's values and appealing pathetically for order while no one took any notice. Slowly the Church came to recognize that it was the Church itself – being small and not taken seriously – that was the child.

Social enterprise

7.30   It is a short – but significant – step from initiating partnerships between communities and local businesses, to developing a vibrant entrepreneurial spirit.

7.31   One positive result of government being open to the contribution of faith communities has been the emergence of a number of social entrepreneurs. The Bromley by Bow Centre in East London came into being when Andrew Mawson, a minister of the United Reformed Church, was invited to a small and rundown church and encouraged to 'dream dreams'. He opened up the space to the community and formed creative partnerships with local people and organizations. Now the centre has 140 staff, an annual turnover of £2 million and 2,000 people passing through each week.

7.32   The centre has developed a distinctive approach to developing and managing integrated community health facilities. It comprises a wide range of statutory health services, community regeneration programmes, arts, education and social enterprise activity, and is regarded as a pioneering organization for social change.

7.33   Meanwhile, Mike Croft, at St Catherine's in Wakefield, decided that the Church had to take action, not just by being on the side of the poor, but by promoting prosperity and empowering local people. Following a fire, St Catherine's was rebuilt not just as a church but also as a conference centre. The church's buildings would be 'made to sweat'. They would become commercially viable, not for the sake of private profit but for the benefit of the community. Profitable parts of the work would be used to support less viable enterprises.

7.34   Such examples illustrate how the churches have found a common interest between their vision for the community and government regeneration programmes. They and other faith communities have accepted the invitation to partnership. Projects like these are found in every town and city – churches working together to meet perceived need and finding funding from charities, health authorities and local businesses.

7.35   But how do small-scale projects become self-sustaining commercial enterprises? Frequently it has been done on a wing and a prayer, funded by the generosity of faithful people who want to see something happen.

7.36   The Government has set up three funds to help:

1)   The Adventure Capital Fund (ACF) is a programme offering community-based organizations three forms of investment:

- Bursaries to help them attract funding for big projects
- Long-term loans with favourable terms
- Time in the form of supporters

The aim is to enable enterprising community organizations to build revenues so that they become independent from traditional sources of funding such as grants, and to fill an investment gap not met by the banks.

2)   Futurebuilders is a £125m Home Office backed investment fund for developing the capacity of the Voluntary and Community Sector (VCS) to deliver public services. Voluntary and community organizations are well placed to deliver certain types of public service, because of their flexibility, community links, specialist knowledge, closeness to users and involvement of volunteers.

However, they often need investment before they can be in a position to tender for contracts or earn fees from public sector agencies.

3) Faith Communities Capacity Building Fund is a 10-year programme launched in September 2005. It is for faith and inter-faith groups and organizations in England and Wales, particularly those in the most disadvantaged area and with the most diverse minority populations. The fund will support capacity building and inter faith activity to increase community cohesion in wider society. Total funding for grants between January 2006 and March 2007 will be up to £5 million. It is expected that small grants will be up to £5,000 and that large grants will be up to £50,000.

Grassroots actions

7.37   There are other patterns of forming partnerships and alliances. Community Organizing, for example, seeks to tap grassroots concerns through intensive one-to-one encounters. The aim is to give people a genuine democratic voice as citizens. Once their concerns have been identified people are equipped to campaign and to form alliances with other groups.

7.38   The model is one of an independent, membership-based alliance of local civil society groups, most of whom, historically, have been faith organizations. The members develop their own agenda aimed at tackling local problems (anything from street lighting to unemployment). These have been identified by listening carefully to the hopes and fears of the people who belong to its member organizations – mosques, churches, schools, trade union branches and community charities. People are then trained how to organize effectively and to be heard by the statutory sector or the business community.

7.39   In this way lasting relationships are built between people of different backgrounds and faiths. The alliances are supported by a small team of professional community organizers who recruit new members to join, run training sessions, and help to move campaigns forward. The strength of the work lies in the broad base of people who work together democratically and with a directed purpose.

7.40   With their well-established structures and long experience of public life in Britain the Christian churches are in a good position to take a lead in this initiative and to invite other faiths to join them. While some congregations will not be interested, others are hungry for ways of being engaged in their cities which give them real freedom to speak and to act as well as the strength to do so effectively.

7.41   Originally inspired by the analysis and vision of *Faith in the City* but drawing also from in the insights of the Industrial Areas Foundation in the United States, Community Organizing (CO) in the UK spent a number of years getting as much wrong as right. Broad based community organizations were set up in a number of British cities which failed to last. However, the lessons of those years have been learned and recent efforts in different areas of London, Birmingham and Sheffield have been more successful.

7.42   At the time of writing, TELCO Citizens in East London was the largest and most consolidated group, Birmingham Citizens was in the initial stages of development, while IMPACT in Sheffield was in a state of suspension following a cessation of Lottery funding. South London Citizens was inaugurated in 2004, and West London Citizens in 2005.

7.43   South London Citizens Enquiry into Lunar House in Croydon, whose campaign is described more fully in Chapter 3, is a prime example of what can be achieved through community organizing. During 2004, the 20 diverse local organizations who belong to South London Citizens undertook a 'Community Listening Campaign' to identify common issues affecting their people. The issues included

Doncaster – home for ex-prisoners
Originally the vision of two Methodist Local Preachers, Rock House in Doncaster is a home for former prisoners, providing accommodation for five men at a time, each staying 6–12 months. It enables them to make a fresh start away from the 'offending environment'. It is backed financially by Housing Benefit, Tudor Trust, Grocery Aid and G. Paul Getty Foundation. The Church Urban Fund pays the salary of the manager.
[B7.3]

lost paperwork, queues for hours in all weathers, and disrespectful treatment at Lunar House, the UK's principal immigration processing centre. As a result of the enquiry set up by South London Citizens, a meeting took place with the Government minister for immigration, Tony McNulty MP, who agreed to co-operate with the implementation of key recommendations.

7.44   There are, however, a number of limitations and obstacles facing community organizing. Very often, only a minority of people within member organizations are actively and regularly engaged. In spite of its 'build from below' philosophy CO has been charged with a concentration of power in the hands of the leaders who do not always get the balance between co-operation and confrontation right. While aiming to be broadly based, such organizations can become top heavy with Christian leaders, and the relationships with other faiths and other community groups can be considerably more fragile than is ideal. Finally, community organizing has a tendency to stand alone from other strands of community development.

7.45   Nevertheless, these are exciting, groundbreaking initiatives. They represent much of what is at the heart of what the Church is meant to be doing to make good cities. And they demonstrate what a careful, prayerful and realistic approach to partnerships can deliver.

Objections, obstacles and risks

7.46   Such vital partnerships between agencies of the state and faith communities as those we have included are full of promise – and risk. We must realistically assess the relationship between faith communities and the state. Can faith communities still speak with an honest and critical voice to those who hold power?

7.47   It is unacceptable if government agencies are seen as the powerful partner – because they bring the money – with the Church simply accepting the Government proscriptions and prescriptions in order to be in partnership. When government holds all the cards it has a 'structural advantage'. It may offer rewards, for example, in the shape of funding to carry out a project, or offer inclusion such as with a seat at the (planning) table. But this may be the equivalent to being co-opted, and being co-opted undermines the ability to critique what is going on. Such a power play is subverted if the Church refuses the blandishments of co-option and, instead, models the way of Jesus and lives with the vulnerable, the weak and the excluded.

7.48   The partnership between government and faith groups can be unequal, potentially distorting the faith groups themselves and fostering conflict between religious traditions. There can be a risk to the integrity of the local church as a distinctive worshipping community if it is channelling more and more energy into maintaining rapidly expanding government sponsored projects.

7.49   The Church should be in partnership with government and others, but unless the partnership is equal, there is a risk that the Church will adopt the Government's or other partners' values in order to remain 'good' partners. Is the Church being coerced into colluding? Should it take a step back and challenge more?

7.50   If the Government and faith communities do not speak the same language, partnership work is hindered. In its document *Working Together*, the Government is explicit in valuing consulting with faith communities. The fact is that *Working Together* has not provided a secure and consistent relationship between faith communities and government at all levels. There needs to be greater clarity over expectations in partnerships. A review of partnership relationships involving faith communities and public authorities should be undertaken jointly, setting out the terms of engagement along the lines of the Government Compact with the Voluntary and Community Sector. We welcome the success of improved police relationships with faith communities and believe it to be a model for other statutory agencies.

7.51   The authors of *'Faith' in Urban Regeneration?*,[7] published by the Joseph Rowntree Foundation, draw attention to the particular difficulties that faith communities have experienced in trying to work with local authorities. A number of their interviewees report a sense that local government has an essentially 'secularist' agenda. They felt that much of local government has still to emerge from a history of paternalism and that pressure from central government is needed to bring about a change of approach.

7.52   It should be pointed out that there are significant numbers of people of faith working in secular regeneration organizations. Nevertheless, the interviews demonstrated that many officials have only a limited awareness of cultural and faith issues. Their religious illiteracy has implications for policy and practice. They therefore sometimes fail to distinguish between ethnic and faith communities. Sikhs are confused with extremist Muslims, liberal Muslims are viewed as fundamentalist, jihadi and misogynist. Reformed Jews are not distinguished from ultra-Orthodox Jews. Evangelical and Pentecostalist Christians are perceived as 'born again fundamentalists' who are inherently right-wing and reactionary. The failure to realize that mosques, gurdwaras, temples and pentecostal missions are not organized on the Anglican parish model adds to an official's problems of locating people with whom they 'can do business'.

7.53   Churches have experienced their own problems with local authorities – not least because there is the desire within the statutory sector to break the monopoly of mainstream Christianity. The Church of England is perceived as well resourced and somehow irrelevant by some officials in high places, whereas the Black Majority Churches receive little acknowledgement for their contribution.

7.54   Mike Crott, a Church of England priest, has pointed out that regeneration and other partnerships with government are hampered by two problems. First, funding regimes are often rigidly short-term – so that a fully functioning project might have to disappear entirely after three years because the grant has expired. And secondly, the expectations loaded upon local projects by governmental bureaucracy are heavy and highly prescriptive. Apart from the quantities of paperwork, there is a tendency for government representatives to claim they know what is best in any circumstances, and to encumber a local initiative with unwelcome or unmanageable features – sometimes including personnel who are poorly equipped for understanding the sensitivities of a locality.

7.55   With the social sector becoming open to the part wealth creation has in regeneration, there is a potential challenge to the private sector, which feels that the world of wealth creation belongs to it. As the social sector is now seen as threatening, grants are being replaced by contracts.

7.56   Both officers and councillors in local authorities are often looking for short-term success. People like these, outside faith communities, do not always understand our commitment to real work and real change, rather than palliative measures simply designed to get people off the unemployment register.

7.57   The reality of regeneration does not always match the claims made for it. The William Temple Foundation, for example, is highly critical of what regeneration schemes have done for Manchester. It said: Manchester's regeneration is heavy on spin and is 'cosmetic'. Levels of poverty, unemployment and health (for example) show few signs of improvement. Regeneration just moves poverty, crime and exclusion to other parts of the city; it doesn't deal with root causes. Those at the top of the organizations believe in the ideas of 'trickle-down/snowball' effects – where benefits gradually work their way 'down' to the poorest people – but there is no firm evidence or long term experience to prove it. Pouring money into poor areas is unpredictable in its effects.

7.58   The churches themselves have some important lessons to learn. Has the Church done enough to help clergy and others at a local level to understand the terminology used by government, or to help them realize the multitude of funds

Hull – drop-in for sex-workers

In Hull, two lay Christian women – one from the Salvation Army and one from a Community Church – became concerned about the number of young women working in prostitution. They set up a drop-in centre, The Lighthouse, which now operates from a bus. It is staffed by people from churches in Hull and supported by Lloyds TSB, Esmee Fairburn Foundation, Church Welfare Association, the Magdelene Trust, Hull and East Riding Association, Sir James Reckitt Charity, Church Urban Fund, British Aerospace, East Riding Health Authority and the Salvation Army.

[B7.6

available via government? Churches must also recognize that entrepreneurial roles do not have to be carried out by the clergy, but could be done by lay leaders. In fact there is a danger that an individual with the capacity to produce major projects accumulates too much power and responsibility. Other churches should note existing training programmes such as the United Reformed Church's training scheme for Church Related Community Workers.

7.59   The whole concept of regeneration excites those whose raison d'être is bound up with an understanding of re-birth and new beginnings, so much so that they may uncritically engage in any programme which seems to offer a fresh start. There is the danger of churches being co-opted to legitimize developments that are driven by the appetites of property developers and that may not be in the interests of local people. For example, redeveloping brown field sites rather than renovating old properties can encourage the development of gated communities – something which is as true of social housing as up-market developments. Churches must also recognize that regeneration has the potential to stir up conflict and competition – as voluntary bodies, tenants groups, churches and mosques compete for resources.

7.60   As this report has already pointed out, faith groups involved in major partnership schemes are faced with a raft of bureaucratic demands for professional standards, which can easily conflict with their own primary purpose. Sometimes projects grow so large that the original sponsoring congregation feel that they have grown out of their reach.

7.61   And uncritical acceptance of public funds can limit the capacity of the Church to be a dissident community, to speak the truth to the very body that is funding its activity.

Plymouth – Mutley Greenbank Trust   [B7.7

Collaboration between three local churches and the two local community associations, led to the development of this Trust, originally financed through the Single Regeneration Budget (SRB). It is chaired by Roger Williams, Vicar of St Matthias, North Hill. All but one of the Trust's agreed SRB outputs were achieved. These included: construction jobs created; training opportunities delivered; young local people worked with; local people given access to new community facilities and volunteering opportunities, community and voluntary groups supported; childcare places created. However, Roger Williams emphasized that for them the 'whole framework came out of the vision of one man', adding that 'without the good fortune in having one very skilled and hardworking individual voluntarily involved, we could never have sustained the task, even of making quarterly returns to the SRB'. In light of this experience, strong representations need to be made to government to simplify the processes involved in accessing and reporting on regeneration money.

Lessons on committed involvement

7.62   Incarnational theology is about translating the divine call to do justice into the ephemeral realities of day to day politics. It calls people, as Jesus Christ put it, to be 'wise as serpents' and 'harmless as doves'.

7.63   To withdraw on the grounds that partnerships involve compromise and getting our hands dirty, only leaves the field open to those to whom getting their hands dirty is less of a problem. To withdraw behind the walls of places of worship, speaking only to one another, is to ignore the divine claim on the whole of creation and the divine invitation to become partners in the redemption of the world. But, if the Church is not to be compromised by partnerships, it must stay true to the core beliefs of its Christian vision. If it is, to use a metaphor of the prophet Isaiah (54.2), 'to lengthen its ropes' through partnership with others, then it must also 'strengthen its pegs' by attention to worship, which touches the heart as well as the mind.

7.64   The Church should not allow too many of its clergy to be diverted from their calling by becoming full-time social entrepreneurs or managers of worthy schemes. While we must thank God for those who have had the vision and the energy to lead the Church down these new paths, the Church must now develop a new cadre of men and women who see this as their vocation.

7.65   The Church must also find new ways of engaging constructively with the private sector to access serious and sustainable investment and high quality performance. However, we need to be clear (in contractual terms also) about what our ethos is and be aware of the predatory nature of 'the market' – good ideas can quickly get stolen.

7.66   But none of this is to say that faith groups should, as a default position, regard partnerships for regeneration with suspicion. We began this chapter by saying that Christians, alongside those of the major historic faiths, live in the hope and possibility of restoration and regeneration.

7.67   We are, in particular, obliged to magnify the plight of the poor and the disadvantaged, and to work towards building a world where poverty is history. In this mission we are committed – indeed glad – to work hand-in-hand with anyone who will share those objectives.

7.68   Faith communities are ideal partners for urban regeneration because they are, as we will explore in the next chapter, present and engaged in some of the country's most deprived communities for the long term. All the more reason why these partnerships should take into account the deep-seated values that faithful capital has to offer, and not be formed simply because of the foothold faith communities offer in hard to reach territories.

8 Grounding and Sustaining Faithful Capital

8.1 Churches have an extensive 'on the ground' presence in poor urban communities throughout the UK. People of faith increasingly show exceptional commitment to neighbourhoods that experience multiple deprivation and the thousands of local faith-based initiatives are practical responses to the pressures that cities experience in a globalizing world.

8.2 Many of these initiatives are seen as a Christian response to need, but this is only half the story. They are also an expression of alternative values to those of mainstream society and culture. They are an 'alternative performance' based on the distinctive values of the Christian faith. Our cities and towns will only flourish if values other than profit, power and status become the drivers of urban change.

8.3 Our contention is that faith-based organizations make a decisive and positive difference to their neighbourhoods through the values they promote, the service they inspire and the resources they command. However, if this distinctive contribution is to be maintained and grow then the mainstream churches must invest more energetically. There needs to be a strategic commitment to retain resources in cities and particularly in poor urban communities and greater imagination and investment in equipping people to make this contribution.

8.4 The impact that churches make in their neighbourhood is now beginning to be recognized – and measured. A 2005 report produced by the Northwest Regional Development Agency[2] estimated that in the Northwest there were 45,667 faith volunteers contributing around 8.1 million volunteer hours per annum. The financial value of this contribution is estimated at between £60.6 million and £64.6 million each year. These volunteer hours amount to 4,815 full-time equivalent jobs.

8.5 The value of civic and communal commitment is unparalleled by any other agency and the Church need have no embarrassment in presenting it more clearly. For example, it is estimated that members of the Church of England:

- Contribute 23.2 million hours voluntary service each month in their local communities in addition to any church commitments.[3]
- A quarter of regular churchgoers are involved in voluntary community service outside the church.[4]
- 108,000 volunteers run activity groups for children and young people associated with their church, providing for 375,000 children (aged 5 to 16 years) and 38,000 young people (aged 16 to 25 years).[5]

8.6 We may flinch at quantifying this commitment in financial terms but, whether we like it or not, this method of ascribing value, prompted by government approaches to evaluation, has become routine. Increasingly, community and voluntary organizations are required by government agencies to account for their work in terms of outcomes and outputs such as the number of 'volunteer hours' generated.

8.7 Given this requirement, the Commission on Urban Life and Faith worked with the Churches Regional Commission for Yorkshire and the Humber to devise the Community Value Toolkit to enable churches to assess the value of their contribution to their neighbourhood. This was undertaken not just in response to the demands of government. Our investigations found that churches in poor communities demonstrate an extensive commitment to engaging, in 'non-churchy' ways, with people in their neighbourhood. The Community Value Toolkit enables churches to 'value' these emerging ways of engaging with people outside the church and to help churches identify the distinctive contributions they make to their community. This then bolsters recognition of 'faithful capital' as a vital but undervalued aspect of social capital.

8.8   In particular, the Community Value Toolkit aims to prevent small congregations – especially in poor areas – from being written off as burdensome and unproductive in their mission. 'To the outsider we are just a small vulnerable group of Christians in a deprived part of the city', explains Liz Henderson, the minister at Richmond Craigmillar Church in Edinburgh. 'Our small numbers mean that we do the traditional things of the church very badly. Our building has Lexan on the windows and graffiti on the walls. But inside there is a community which is rich because of its faith. The projects we run offer other people the opportunity to touch that and glimpse what lies inside.'

> ## 'We do it differently because we're the Church'　[B8.1]
>
> ### How one Christian community has responded to grief in a neighbourhood
>
> Members of Richmond Craigmillar Church in Edinburgh opened a café within the church building. Jessie Douglas, a local person was employed to run the café. Jessie's son had died in a motorbike accident a year and a half before the café opened and from the café's earliest days people came in with stories from their lives – stories of children living with drug-addicted parents, stories of housing difficulties and stories of loss. Stories of loss became increasingly common as we faced a series of tragic deaths in our community.
>
> Most of the losses have been tragic – children who have lost parents or other relatives in car accidents and through suicide and murder – and people began to ask if they could sit in the church for a while on their own. Eventually, people asked if they could have a memorial to the people who had died and a group drawn from the church and the wider community decided to make a tree out of copper piping. People learned how to weld and cut leaves out of copper sheets. While the copper tree was being made a boy of thirteen died in an accident at home. It was a devastating for his parents and five brothers and sisters. Soon after, three children, Louise and Calais and Lewis came in to the café, their parents had been killed in a road accident. From these and other experiences a second project was born – a child bereavement project, Richmond's Hope, which gives children a chance to express in therapeutic play the feelings associated with their loss.
>
> Richmond's Hope is for children of all faiths and none.

Church buildings are more than bricks and mortar

8.9   The importance of places of worship – the buildings themselves – can also be underestimated. There is now incontrovertible evidence that church buildings can be transformed into convivial and significant spaces in urban areas. The skill to adapt and use these buildings in imaginative ways is now widely available. That said, the financial resources to undertake modification to church buildings can be daunting.

8.10   With property developers ever alert to the profit available from capturing urban sites, the significance of a church building should not be underestimated. As well as having a powerful symbolic presence, church buildings may be the last remaining communal space within a neighbourhood – in which case, however deep the pockets of the developer, to the local neighbourhood such buildings might be priceless. They are also bold beacons of resistance against

> 'The copper tree is a visual symbol of all that we do because we are the church and we do it differently because we are the Church. We pray for the people who come to the café and Richmond's Hope. Often you will find someone sitting in the church because they want to – and because they find it helps them to be there.'
> Liz Henderson

the blandness and commercial routine of so many town centres and High Streets. They are major contributors to a 'sense of place', something vital to the streetscape which is now being recognized by town planners. One of the most notable and perhaps overlooked roles that church buildings play in town and city centres is simply as places of calm and tranquillity, a refuge from the hustle and bustle of modern life. This is something that Malcolm McClaren, the punk rock svengali behind The Sex Pistols, observed in an interview: 'Church is the most fantastic place. It's sanctuary. They should be open 24 hours a day. They're the only place left in London where you don't have to buy anything.'

8.11   Away from town centres, church buildings can provide significant spaces for sanctuary or community in areas in estate neighbourhoods that have suffered from poor design and the demise of community facilities.

8.12   *Building Faith in Our Future*, a report produced by the Church Heritage Forum[6] explores in detail how church buildings contribute positively to the life of a neighbourhood. Research[7] suggests that:

- 86% of the adult population had been in their local church/ place of worship in the previous year. This was primarily to mark social rites of passage (births, marriages and deaths) and important Christian cultural festivals (for example, Christmas, Easter, Remembrance Day, Mothering Sunday) – but 19%, that is 1 in 5, were seeking a quiet space.[8]
- The Church of England alone provides over 16,000 buildings for local community use. On average, every year local congregations spend over £112,000 on major repairs to these buildings.
- 63% of people would be concerned if their local church/chapel was not there. This includes 38% of those with no religion or of faiths other than Christianity.[9]

8.13   We would strongly advocate an opportunistic approach to church buildings, especially in poor urban areas, which must not be portrayed as millstones that compete with or undermine purposeful mission. The sheer existence of a church in a locality establishes a certain potential. This is aptly illustrated by St Leonard's Church in Bilston in the West Midlands (see box B8.3), an early driver of the major regeneration programme in the area.

In the 2005 Opinion Research Business survey, sponsored by the Archbishops' Council and English Heritage:

- *58 % agreed with the statement 'places of worship make our neighbourhood a better place to live' while 11% disagreed.*
- *72 % agreed with the statement 'a place of worship is an important part of the local community' while 11% disagreed.*
- *72 % agreed with the statement 'places of worship provide valuable social and community facilities' while 11% disagreed.*
- *Among respondents who claimed no religious allegiance, 38%, 46% and 56%, respectively, agreed with the statements.*

The importance of churches to local communities is further supported in the survey by the desire of respondents for even more from their places of worship:

- *63% agreed with the statement 'places of worship should be more actively involved in our local community' while 13% disagreed.*
- *69% agreed with the statement 'places of worship should be more accessible to the local community' while 8% disagreed. [10]*

[B8.2

How one parish church found a new way of ministering

Bilston in the West Midlands, once a prosperous steel town, suffered a body blow with the closure of most of the nearby heavy industry. It almost took the heart out of St Leonard's, the parish church, too. 'Twenty years of low wages and unemployment had had a visible impact,' explains the local vicar Chris Thorpe. 'To an outside eye, the town looked run-down, tatty and depressed. And church attendances and income had declined, with increasingly elderly congregations. The future looked uncertain for the parish of Bilston.'

In 1995 the congregation decided to research the needs of local people. Door-to-door interviews at over 2,000 households took place. The research showed two concerns not being addressed:

- *The needs of young people*
- *The isolation and vulnerability of elderly people*

As a direct result, a proactive telephone support service for elderly people – Senior Citizen Link Line – was developed, and after just three years, over 1,000 people were being supported through the link line. For some it was 'just to talk', while other conversations led to advocacy such as helping people to receive a proper level of service or responding to gaps in provision. One spin-off was a local building firm providing their work force to help with lifting work such as bringing a bed downstairs so that someone could come home from hospital. A 'Care and Repair' service was set up for smaller tasks. The Link Line exposed the number of elderly people who had been victims of crime which they had not reported and links were made with the police and perpetrators have been apprehended.

When the Church Urban Fund provided a pump-priming grant, this opened doors to other sources of funds. From this small beginning, the last ten years have seen the following developments:

- *Extension of the Link Line to the whole of Wolverhampton with the support of the Big Lottery Fund, now to be further extended through the Primary Care Trust*
- *The church being opened each day because those being phoned wanted to meet the people who rang. This in turn led to opening the Melting Pot Café in the church, attracting over a 1,000 visitors in the first year*
- *Recreation classes in the open church*
- *A prayer chapel, used daily by local people*
- *Quality Concerts, including by the City of Birmingham Symphony Orchestra*
- *The Link Line call centre has now developed a training arm (Tele Resources Limited) to equip and train local people in response to the growing industry of call centres in the Black Country, placing nearly 70 young people into full-time jobs in the first year*
- *Support for the Link Line – as Tele Resources Ltd has become an invaluable resource for local undertakers enabling them to ensure the availability of clergy to conduct funerals*

8.14   By harnessing the perspectives and expertise of social enterprise a building can be transformed from liability into asset. The potential to make that building 'sweat' in the way exemplified by St Leonard's, Bilston, St Catherine's, Wakefield, the Bromley-by Bow Centre in London's East End, to name three examples, is increasingly recognized. Such an entrepreneurial approach, which develops income through trading and contracting without damaging the church's central charitable intent, is legitimized by the advent of Community Interest Companies.[11] We commend this new legal structure to churches and associated initiatives as a means of enabling church buildings to be harnessed for the benefit of the local community in a sustainable way.

8.15   In most European nations, including secular France, church buildings receive substantial government subsidy. In Britain, day-to-day running and maintenance of church buildings is the responsibility of the congregation and other well wishers. Ironically, research[12] suggests, that the majority of people in Britain are ignorant of this and assume the Government pays for the upkeep of church buildings. The recent granting of VAT relief on listed buildings is greatly welcomed, and we commend the ongoing dialogue between government and the Church on the cost and significance of buildings.

In it for the long term

8.16   But it is at least in part due to the availability of buildings that faith communities have, in comparison with other 'voluntary' and community groups, significantly greater longevity. This long-term presence within a neighbourhood enables churches to give what the Archbishop of Canterbury calls 'patient attention'[13] to people and to the issues that impact on their lives.

8.17   Such 'close to the ground' commitment is a major dividend of faithful capital, providing perspectives and opportunities that are not easily available to agencies that 'look in' from the outside.

Letting their voices be heard   [B8.4

Since January 2000, REGENERATE.com in Roehampton has been running a lunch club for elderly people who live on the Alton estate SW London. The project was set up to demonstrate friendship, love and care particularly to elderly people living in isolation. The project was set up with financial support from Wandsworth Borough Council but in February 2004, REGENERATE.com received a letter from the council saying that they didn't see lunch clubs as a priority any more and that funding was to be stopped to all lunch clubs for the elderly. This provoked real fury among the 100 or so members of the Roehampton lunch club who had come to depend upon the service not just for hot meals but for new friendships.

'The following week,' writes Andy Smith of Regenerate, 'we took 100 elderly people down to the town hall and blocked the Wandsworth one-way system by sitting everyone around tables and chairs in the road. 'The traffic was blocked by about seven minibuses and the elderly people brought their banners and their voices. The hundred pensioners sat around their tables with their plates, knives and forks but with no food as a visual picture of what would happen without the small amount of money that the council had decided to pull. The demo lasted an hour, council officials were fuming, traffic was building, the public gave the pensioners their vocal support, a petition got over 4,000 signatures and ripples were made. It didn't do enough to make the council fund the project, but it has increased our passion to maintain a service that changes lives. We have continued the lunch club as part of our RISE (Reaching ISolated Elderly) project and also set up another one down the road in Putney.'

One of the most powerful contributions of faith communities to contemporary social fabric is one of its least-noticed – simply being there. This was something Commissioners discovered when they visited Hull and Newcastle. As one of our Commissioners noted:

'We saw love in action as people work together for the good of their neighbourhoods, often struggling with the task but seeing amazing things happen. They continue with this work, without much recognition, local people who want to remain local but who quite often want to run away from it too. It is obvious that they have discovered that love for their neighbourhood is hard, sometimes thankless, sometimes life threatening and sometimes rewarding. We saw love in the dedicated workers and volunteers, people whose struggles have lasted for years, people whose determination keeps them going from day to day, people who out of love for God and for their neighbour dream the possible and strive to make it happen.

The team vicar of Marfleet, Hull, Canon Suzanne Sheriff is a case in point. She's working in a parish church that isn't magnificent. The church building could do with refurbishing but they have no funds to do it and she says she's not really bothered about doing so. She prefers to spend her time doing 'important' things like helping people to cope with the everyday traumas that happen in this area.

Her church is at the heart of a community that struggles to survive and the building reflects the area. Every day in the parish is different and she spends many hours listening to people whose lives are fragile to say the least. She told us stories of desperate parents whose children were enticed into crime, she told stories of family arguments and runaway children, she told us stories of drug abuse.

Despite the lack of facilities they started an afternoon club for the local children. She didn't have extra workers and so encouraged the parents to stay at the club. She began to tell stories from the Bible, the parents began to take an interest and now she has as many parents as children attending the club.

She loves the place where she is present and engaged. She loves the people she is working with, her stamina is amazing, her commitment total.

The 'moral sense' of people of faith – an alternative value system

8.18   Underlying the stories of people of faith who have organized themselves and the wider community in social action are a rich seam of values, principles and perspectives born of that faith. Grant makers and policy makers have a tendency to distinguish between the 'social provision' made by churches and the proclamation of the faith I.e. proselytizing. This distinction fails to do justice to the 'moral sense', which is also promoted by people of faith. The quotation from the Chief Rabbi, which opens Chapter 1, comes from his Smith Institute lecture on 'The Moral Sense'. This 'moral sense' gives value to things such as honesty, self-effacement, generosity of spirit, putting others' needs ahead of one's own and genuine respect for those who know deeply about personal distress and struggle. Our case is that it is this 'moral sense', maintained by religious teaching and religious discipline, which proves such a potent source of transformation of individuals and neighbourhoods. This is widely overlooked or misunderstood.

8.19   Senior citizens from high-rise estates in Roehampton will have felt an aspect of this in the annual Kings and Queens party for pensioners hosted by 'Regenerate' in South London. 'Nearly 500 people turn up,' explains Andy Smith of Regenerate. 'It takes place in a large marquee and we provide a top-quality three-course meal, fine wines and ales, a beautiful arrangement of flowers and entertainment. The message to the elderly in our community is that we value them and love them and God loves them and values them. We aim to treat them like Kings and Queens for a day. For many people, the party is the highlight of their year. "The best day of my life!" was how one person put it.'

8.20   Not only do we seek to commend the 'moral sense' that is fostered by the involvement of people of faith in their neighbourhood, we also maintain that religious faith is, in itself, an essential resource which enables people to take charge of their lives, especially when they have to struggle with addiction or isolation or poverty. It has the capacity to help people find inner transformation, not simply to alter their outside circumstances. But reluctance to allow people of faith to speak of the motivation behind their commitment to those who experience exclusion risks inhibiting vital resources that are beneficial to urban life.

8.21   It is Christian faith that inspires The Community Action Team (CAT) initiative in Bradford, part of the outreach of the Abundant Life Church. This is a multi-ethnic congregation of 2,500 which supports a diverse range of community initiatives including 'red-light ministry, prison ministry, mobile food and clothing' and help to the homeless, they told the Commission: 'We equip and resource teams of ordinary but appropriately skilled volunteers to work diligently and relationally, serving the people in our communities. 'With a heart of love, we aim to help the forgotten, neglected and hurting people of Bradford through self-help programmes, helping them to develop their life and social skills.'[14]

8.22   The stories, scriptures, songs, prayers, rituals and teachings that form the everyday life of religious faith (the 'habits of the heart') are not some anthropological curiosity. They are the source of the values which prompt action on behalf of those who are marginalized. The practices of faith and the actions of the faithful on behalf of their neighbour cannot be separated.

8.23   The Commission is convinced that the practical application and the dissemination of the values, born of the 'moral sense' that emanates from the world's religions, are viable and relevant to the demands of a globalizing world. With the Chief Rabbi we argue that moral sense needs to be explicitly 'acquired, nurtured and sustained' in our faith communities.[15] The significance of the inspiration brought by faith should not be undervalued or dismissed because of the disruption caused by those few who use religion as a reason to reject those who are different or to legitimate violence or oppression.

8.24   As more local authorities appoint specialist 'Faith Officers' this should enable them to understand better the 'moral sense' that is integral to the major religious faiths, and which means that it is unreasonable to distinguish between the social action undertaken by people of faith and the values and approaches which they embrace.

Intentional commitment

8.25   One of the most interesting developments to emerge over the last 20 years has been an increasing number of 'intentional' communities, especially in poor urban areas. These initiatives enable people of faith to express a lifestyle which some call a 'new monasticism'. For example, the Hope Community in Heath Town, Wolverhampton emerged not long after the publication of *Faith in the City*. An established Roman Catholic Community, the Sisters of the Infant Jesus, responded to the call to work among those with the least resources and as a result moved into a flat on an estate (see box B8.6). There are now a number of 'hope communities' on housing estates in the Midlands.

8.26 A growing number of such intentional communities express similar radical commitment in cities across the UK, especially in poor neighbourhoods.[17] Sometimes residential, they tend to attract younger Christians and sometimes members of the 'order' work in order to support others who undertake full-time ministry. There are now sufficient examples to identify some defining characteristics of these sustained expressions of radical discipleship. They:

- have a structure that enables a deeper commitment (a total lifestyle informed by gospel values) than is usually expressed by membership of a local church;
- are responsive to local challenges;
- emphasize both devotion and active involvement;
- have flexible arrangements to enable people both to join and to leave;
- build an 'esprit-de-corps';
- maintain a positive relationship to a local church, although the vocation of the group is not necessarily expressed through the church.

8.27 A number of intentional communities, especially those in major cities, are becoming adept at creating what are known as 'proximity spaces' - places or events where people who are quite different from one another can interact in an atmosphere that encourages talk about faith, values, and shared concerns. This might be a flat available for community use in a tower block, a café, a nightclub, an art gallery or library. The challenge to longstanding local churches is to rejoice in the exceptional commitment that is emerging in so many diverse expressions.

The Church Urban Fund - distinctive, effective, influential

8.28 Founded as a direct result of *Faith in the City*, the Church Urban Fund is essential to the responsiveness and health of churches in poor urban communities. Such independent funding is vital if the imagination of people of faith is to develop in ways that energize the 'alternative performance' to which faith communities are called. The commitment of the Church Urban Fund to draw alongside groups that are still in their 'setting-up' phase has done much to encourage those making the first steps towards community engagement. It has also proved to have been remarkably effective stewardship. For example, the £4.5 million awarded to over 365 community projects in Southwark Diocese has resulted in a further £30 million from other sources.[18]

8.29 Not only does the Church Urban Fund invest in groups that are in the early stage of development, it has also been willing to allocate sufficient funds to make the payment of a salary feasible. Government departments and other grant makers could learn much from the practice of the Church Urban Fund.

8.30 The experience that the Church Urban Fund has gleaned in relation to groups that are motivated by a faith commitment would also be valuable to draw on. Even to the extent of being harnessed by Government departments and agencies to provide a channel through which funding can be delivered to faith groups.

Fostering healthy faith

8.31 The presence of a building or a congregation does not, of itself, guarantee an outward looking approach. The Church of England report, *Presence and Engagement* says:

> If being present is a necessary condition for engagement, it is certainly not sufficient. The increasing fluidity and change in the physical and social environment and the loss of familiar faces and landmarks can lead to powerful pressures towards holding fast to whatever remains of what

A revolution in kindness
'Change will always come about by a group of moral dissenters and the persistence of small committed groups of people willing to fail over long periods of time, until that rare wonderful moment when the dam of oppression, indifference and greed finally cracks and those in power finally accept what the world's people have been saying all along – that there has to be a revolution in kindness.'
Anita Roddick

was a huddling together and a reinforcement of an inward looking attitude. In a determination faithfully to remain present, local churches can become increasingly an isolated presence, grimly hanging on, but largely unrelated to the surrounding context from which they become increasingly estranged. Churches can be present without being engaged and it requires a constant commitment to move on from being present to also being engaged.[19]

8.32   Churches with fearful congregations can become the ecclesiastical equivalents of gated communities and such isolation and inward looking churches add little to the flourishing of a city. In contrast, healthy, life-giving faith which can be relied on to contribute to the flourishing of the city will have the following hallmarks:

- **It will enlarge our imagination:** by setting the story of our lives in the framework of a much larger story than ourselves which gives our life coherence, meaning, purpose and direction.
- **It will teach and encourage the practice of wisdom and holiness:** finding our happiness and fulfilment is about coming to a right understanding of who we are, and what it means to be mature human being in terms of vulnerability as well as potential.
- **It will open us up to the new:** while religion continues to be a profoundly important vehicle for personal and community identity it also embraces a humility borne of the awareness that our knowledge is partial – we see through a glass only darkly. Healthy religion gives confidence to embrace the stranger and insights that are available from those with a different experience of life.
- **It will deepen our sympathies:** it unlocks our compassion because it sees the whole of humankind sharing in a common unfolding story.

8.33   These hallmarks of a faith that can openly engage with a globalizing world also indicate the kind of tools and resources that local faith communities need to be equipped with. For example, Christians living in areas where a significant proportion of the population is drawn from other faiths need equipping to enable them to rise above resentment and to achieve cordial relationships. Christians will not be alone in relation to this. Most others in that neighbourhood will be in a similar position.

8.34   Capacity building is concerned with providing this essential equipment. It is a term which is used particularly in relation to the regeneration of poor neighbourhoods and towns and cities. It means providing skills, resources, confidence and a voice in order to enable to effect change. If we are to promote flourishing communities, we believe the prevailing approach to capacity building needs to be enlarged to enable people to reflect on the 'micro' ways in which people relate to each other, and to gain skills in relation to this. These 'micro' ways in which people relate to each other can be shaped by the values and practices of religious faith, proving vital in a successful neighbourhood regeneration strategy. This would introduce concepts such as:

- Grace
- Generosity of spirit
- Giving priority to those who have least power
- Awareness of our inclination to accumulate and hoard power and influence – and ways of counteracting this
- Forgiveness

Theological education in an urban context

8.35   This Commission endorses the importance of theological education as a means of equipping and building up the Christian community. We strongly support initiatives in urban theological training that focus on the local context, which encourage participants to reflect theologically on their experience and which build up a variety of ministries for the people of God. This ranges from ordained stipendiary ministry, church related community ministries, to forms of accredited lay ministry through to opportunities for people of faith located in 'secular' contexts such as local government or the voluntary sector. We regard such provision as a vital part of the task of building up the 'faithful capital' of local communities through effective education and training. We therefore welcome the growing number of initiatives that enable people of faith to make sense of their social engagement in a rapidly changing urban environment. Examples include:

- The School of Urban Mission in London and Liverpool, developed through co-operation between the Regeneration Trust and the Church Army
- The Inter-Cultural Communication Leadership School which enables people of different faiths to be trained together in relation to community leadership
- Genetik, the innovative training course being established for young people by 'The Message' to help lay people in particular
- The Urban Theology Unit, Sheffield, with a long term commitment to 'urban vocation' through training, incarnational presence, and post-graduate research
- Urban Presence in Manchester, a catalyst for the release of resources to enable, equip and encourage Christians living and working in urban areas.[20]

8.36   The relative speed with which these initiatives are set up presents a challenge to those who invest in the established processes of ministerial training. In particular, they make for a stark contrast to the mechanics set in train by the Hind Report,[21] which calls for better co-ordination and co-operation between denominations and institutions concerned with formal theological training.

8.37   The development of Regional Training Partnerships is at different stages in different parts of the country. These provide the opportunity to pool resources and work ecumenically in order to ensure that training for urban ministry gets represented and promoted in this emerging environment.

8.38   At a meeting of theological educators convened by the Commission, we found evidence that the situation had not moved on significantly since *Faith in the City*. Urban-based theological placements were still competing for space in over-crowded timetables. And the practical, contextual and locally based elements of training often took second place to aspects of the formal curriculum that were judged more 'academic'.

8.39   Theology' and 'practice' must be held together. Too often students spend limited time in an urban context and return to their institution to reflect theologically on their experience. This gives the mistaken impression that theology only takes place in an academic context. Similarly, local placements frequently fail to draw on the skills of local leadership, so that local congregations are regarded as 'guinea pigs' rather than 'partners' in the learning process.

8.40   We need a fresh approach to ministerial training with thinking which is 'outside the ecclesiastical box'. We recommend that innovative patterns of training – involving collaborative work between colleges and courses, students and local people – be encouraged. One possibility might be to develop programmes of 'enquiry-based' or 'problem-based' learning such as those used in medical, nursing, engineering and other professional training.[22]

8.41   Despite numerous efforts over the last 20 years, the pattern of training for urban ministry remains fragmented, and good initiatives in one area are often not communicated and taken up elsewhere. All too frequently, Christian denominations do not share resources or best practice as fully as they should. Similarly, links with secular agencies and training opportunities, especially those associated with regeneration and renewal initiatives, are underdeveloped. So too are the cross-disciplinary research opportunities in Higher Education.

8.42   We would like to see an ecumenical network of urban theological education developed, possibly by the creation of a national point of exchange for urban and contextual theology. Such an exchange would aim to enable a diversity of local initiatives to flourish while offering a 'critical mass' of expertise and best practice. It might also facilitate a national framework of accreditation and validation, leading to a variety of qualifications.

8.43   We also strongly believe that a significant element of theological education in urban contexts should be training for the increasingly diverse and multi-faith environments. We commend the work done in Leicester (see box B8.8) by Andrew Wingate and others as an example of what might emerge.

8.44   We also recognize the emerging use of the language of 'spirituality' in many urban professions such as urban planning, management and sociology, and the introduction of provision of 'spiritual care' in health care, education and other public services. There is a growing need for resources and training in this area and for greater critical examination of what is meant by 'spirituality' in secular and religious contexts. We welcome initiatives such as the Manchester Centre for Urban Spirituality, jointly sponsored by the Anglicans and Methodists – and supported by secular partners – which aims to provide training, space for reflection and research for those seeking to explore dimensions of their spiritual development.

8.45   We endorse what *Faith in the City* had to say about the core objectives of theological training and regard these as a continuing powerful statement of how clergy and laity together need to be equipped practically and theologically. The report stated: 'What matters is whether they have developed habits of reflection and social awareness such that they can draw creatively on their resources of theology and spirituality in the face of new realities and engage in a dialogue with those of other faiths and none.'[23]

Urban Ministry and Theology Project [B8.8]

The Urban Ministry and Theology Project (UMTP), based in the East End of Newcastle, sees itself as a resource for the local church, working to build up existing urban Christian congregations numerically, spiritually and theologically. Some of its aims are: 'to create a setting where local people, Church and non-Church, can share what they have learnt about discovering God in the East End of Newcastle with each other and with people who come to learn. That those who come in and those who are already there learn from each other. That together we can seek justice in the regeneration of our City, Church and country.'

UMTP has three core strands:
- *Community engagement*
- *Church development (including new ways of being church)*
- *Theological reflection*

It works to establish strategic partnerships between the communities of the East End, churches and statutory and voluntary agencies. It seeks to ensure that 'local Christians are developing models of ministry that arise directly out of the context of social and economic regeneration'.

It is also concerned to ensure that 'those engaged in theological training, for lay and ordained ministries and in continuing ministerial education, are able both to share in the learning gained by local people and to make a significant contribution'.

This is therefore a 'bottom-up' model of doing theology, in which the practical challenges facing local communities form the agenda for further action and reflection. The focus is on using the resources of Christian education, life-long learning and urban theology to facilitate effective ministry in a local context.[24]

Re-thinking faithful leadership

8.46 Developing the habit of reflection and social awareness and drawing on the resources of theology and spirituality are important tools in avoiding burn-out. As local churches become more engaged in their neighbourhood, the repertoire of skills required by clergy widens, increasing the risk of stress and exhaustion. Our consultations lead us to commend (alongside appropriately informed programmes of continuing education) a number of practices that can reduce the likelihood of burn-out:

- Promoting reflective ministry and making provision for non-managerial supervision;
- Using psychometric tests to get insight into where one is in relation to burn-out and to help put together ministry teams;
- Resisting the inclination to put inexperienced clergy in stressful locations.

8.47 The Commission believes we cannot keep widening the role of 'ministers' of religion, whether they be priests, imams, rabbis or ministers. It is now necessary to invest in roles other than those of minister or priest, specialist roles which could operate across denominational and even faith boundaries. Furthermore, the creation of additional roles offers scope to appoint someone from a different faith. And experience suggests that the presence of a member of staff from another faith contributes greatly to increased understanding both of another faith and one's own.

8.48 As more specialist community ministries have begun to emerge, the training and networking of those who take on specialist roles is a priority. It would be wasteful for this to be undertaken by each denomination. We acknowledge the significant work undertaken by the National Churches Estate Network in supporting and equipping those who minister on housing estates. In other areas of work, mechanisms need to be devised to enable a collaboration approach, which can also harness the contribution of Black-led churches.

8.49 As government, both at national and local levels, seeks to talk with 'faith communities', the processes of consultation will require a representative group. Local Councils of Churches may sometimes be disparaged but they are the best body we have to undertake this role. Churches in our cities and towns need to debate how they are to represent themselves to public bodies that seek to offer people of faith a seat at the table and the status of 'stakeholder'. Too often the faith agenda has been interpreted as relating only to minority faith communities.

8.50 The established denominations must be alert to the relevance and innovation associated with the energy and extensiveness of Black-led churches in many cities. We need to give more focused attention to developing a more robust and creative foundation for future relationships.

8.51 The contribution of supplementary schools,[25] mainly resourced by Black-led churches, is a response to the challenge of young people who are perceived as failing educationally. The stories of success from supplementary schools are rarely acknowledged, yet they contribute immensely to the well-being of young black people. There is a strong case for these schools to receive more significant and consistent funding in their role of working alongside local schools to support young people who might otherwise fail to achieve their potential.

St Philip's Centre for Theology and Ministry in a Multi-Faith Society, Leicester

Located in a refurbished set of church buildings in the heart of a thriving Muslim, Sikh and Hindu area of the city, St Philip's Centre provides a focus for evening classes, day workshops and longer residential courses aimed at fostering inter-faith dialogue and facilitating education and training for Christian ministers based in multi-faith areas. The Centre encourages participants to reflect on the implications of a multi-faith society from the perspective of issues such as asylum-seeking, family life, education and young people. It also provides training for leaders from voluntary and statutory agencies keen to know more about the role of faith-based organizations in their city.

[B8.9

Authentic engagement: why the 'local' matters more than ever

8.52   Our consultations have left us in no doubt that local initiatives and the diverse voices they raise need to be valued more highly. In a fragmenting world, efforts to manage things from the centre are likely to be expensive and ineffective. This puts a premium on a consistent, outward-looking presence on the ground.

8.53   In a world where global forces are driven by the narrow values of profit, power and status, there is little scope for consideration of the 'common good'. Therefore, the many local stories that have been gathered by the Commission are examples of a renewal of social organization and justice in the face of what would otherwise be fierce, and determining global dynamics. These local stories are attempts at articulating what is the common good in a particular neighbourhood or city.

8.54   We call upon the Church of England and other denominations to exercise a fierce commitment to staying in the urban communities of our nation and to contribute in every way possible to the flourishing of our cities. When we express our determination that faith should have a role at a local level in bringing 'good news to the poor' we are not referring simply to providing a care service for the victims of poverty, exclusion or misfortune. We want people of faith to contribute their distinctive values in sharing development of a physical and spiritual environment which makes a good city and which fosters the deep well-being of its citizens.

8.55   The language of renewal, regeneration and renaissance speak of the spiritual dimension in the reordering of our cities. It is a theological language which recognizes the divine involvement in, and concern for, every aspect of human life. Every day, across the country, people are profoundly involved in the healing and transformation of their neighbourhoods. It is their vision and faithfulness that gives us the courage to celebrate life and faith in our urban communities and commit ourselves to calling for justice for all.

Recommendations

W e have gathered our Commission's recommendations together here for easy reference but they emerge from the arguments we have set out in the body of the report itself.

The report was commissioned by the Church of England, so some recommendations are specifically addressed to this institution and its members, but we believe they are also of relevance to other responsible bodies within churches and faith communities.

We make recommendations to the Government and other agencies, but there are occasions where we have not been able to specify the most appropriate body. We make our observations and for the sake of the well-being of our cities these need to be taken up.

Faithful capital

1. The Church of England with its ecumenical partners must maintain a planned, continued and substantial presence across our urban areas.

Implications

1. In relation to buildings, local leadership must be empowered to enable the creation of robust local structures, which can decide how to select and resource the best buildings for the purpose of worship and community needs.
2. We commend the use of the Community Value Toolkit as a resource for making decisions about the availability and deployment of human resources.
3. Government agencies should provide 'easy to access' grants to subsidize the heating costs of buildings used for community benefit, using sustainable energy resources.
4. The refunding of VAT should extend beyond listed buildings to include those in poor neighbourhoods who are receiving regeneration budgets.
5. Churches must take a lead on cherishing our public space and the natural environment of our urban areas.

2. Leaders in all situations need to have the opportunity of exposure to urban and contextual theology and practice.

Implications

1. Opportunities for training and development in urban ministry, lay and ordained, should be fully integrated into the churches' formal training and accreditation and, wherever possible, be done ecumenically.
2. We commend the Church Related Community Worker initiative established by the United Reformed Church and ask that it be extended so that the training modules are available to other denominations and faith related community workers.
3. Recruitment, training and continuing development of church leaders, clerical and lay, should give priority to their ability to empower others. In particular there is a priority to encourage engagement with others in public life.
4. Church and faith communities should together set up an Urban Policy Forum to monitor and address issues relating to urban life and faith.
5. We welcome the Government initiative to establish the Academy for Sustainable Communities and ask that the contribution of faith is included in its thinking.

Wealth and poverty

3. For the flourishing of a just and equitable society the gap between those living in poverty and the very wealthy must be reduced.

Implications

1. The Government is asked to consider the effects of implementing a living wage rather than a minimum wage.
2. The Government should expand the criteria it uses for measuring economic success by including the Measure of Domestic Progress developed by the New Economics Foundation.
3. We commend initiatives being taken to involve people who experience poverty in the solution to problems in their community. We commend pilot schemes such as 'Participatory Budgeting' and the Sustainable Livelihoods programmes.
4. While government must do more to tackle the inequalities, the churches also have a duty to challenge the thoughtless accumulation of wealth which ignores the needs of the poor, both globally and locally. Churches must not hold back from confronting selfish lifestyles either in their own membership or in the wider population.

Equity in diversity

4. Social cohesion depends on the ability of people to live in harmony. Faith groups in particular must combat racism, fascism and religious intolerance at all levels of society.

Implications

1. Churches and faith groups must express gracious hospitality through bonding, bridging and linking.
2. An essential aspect of engagement in contemporary society is the development of networks between faith communities and secular communities. Examples of good practice should be identified and disseminated for wider learning.
3. The development of organizations such as the Interfaith Network, the Council for Christians and Jews, the Christian/Muslim Forum should be supported financially and their insights used by both faith groups and Government departments.
4. We commend Community Organizing and Community Development practice as ways of addressing local needs and issues of justice and in encouraging shared actions.

5. The Government must lead rather than follow public opinion on immigration, refugee and asylum policy. Specifically, asylum seekers should be allowed to sustain themselves and contribute to society through paid work. It is unacceptable to use destitution as a tool of coercion when dealing with 'refused' asylum seekers.

Partnership

6. There needs to be greater clarity over expectations in partnership relationships between faith communities and public authorities at national, regional and local level.

Implications

1. A major review of partnership relationships involving faith communities should be undertaken by Government agencies and faith communities as a means to ensure better and more consistent practice.
2. Churches and faith communities should ensure that there are regional arrangements to publicize, service and monitor partnership schemes in their areas and seek government support.
3. Partnership agreements should include long term implications of short term funding arrangements and the coverage of core operational costs. Government at all levels needs to take into account the distress and disruption caused to small voluntary and community organizations continually having to secure funding.

Young people

7. Government and faith communities must give new consideration to the informal education of young people.

Implications

1. The statutory nature of the Youth Service must be reinstated and properly funded by local authorities.
2. Key worker status must be given to youth work practitioners so they are recruited and retained in urban areas.
3. The spiritual well-being of young people must be an essential part of the Youth Matters strategy and implementation.
4. Young people's Councils of Faith should be developed and resourced to build respect and encourage participation in civic society.

8. We recommend a review of the role and impact of faith schools on social and community cohesion in urban settings.

Church Urban Fund

9. The Church of England should continue to support the Church Urban Fund as a vital resource for the churches' engagement in urban life.

10. Other denominations that have funds to support community engagement are asked to consider seriously whether they should work in partnership with the Church Urban Fund rather than maintaining separate structures.

What makes a good city?

11. Church leaders are asked to initiate wide ranging national debates about what makes a good city in light of this report.

Notes

Chapter 1 Faithful Cities: Places of Celebration, Vision and Justice

1.   James Q. Wilson and Jonathan Sacks, *The Moral Sense*, London: The Smith Institute, 2002, p. 15.

2.   Leonie Sandercock, *Towards Cosmopolis*, London: John Wiley, 1998, p. 198.

3.   J. Field, *Social Capital*, London: Routledge, 2003, p. 1.

4.   Here, we are drawing on the idea of 'religious capital' developed in: C. Baker and H. Skinner, *Telling the Stories: How the Churches are Contributing to Social Capital*, Manchester: William Temple Foundation, 2005.

5.   R. Furbey, A. Dinham, R. Farnell, D. Finneron with C. Howarth, D. Hussain, S. Palmer and G. Wilkinson, *Faith as Social Capital: Connecting or Dividing?*, Bristol: The Policy Press, 2006.

6.   Chris Baker and Hannah Skinner, *Telling the Stories: How Churches are Contributing to Social Capital*, Manchester: William Temple Foundation, 2004, available at http://www.wtf.org.uk/research.html

7.   *Income, Wealth and Inequalities*, House of Commons Library, Research Paper 04/70, 15 September 2004.

8.   Doreen Massey, 'Living in Wythenshawe' in I. Borden, J. Kerr, J. Rendell and A. Piraro (eds), *The Unknown City: Contesting Architecture and Social Space*, MIT Press, 2001.

9.   Duncan Forrester, *Apocalypse Now?: Reflections on Faith in a Time of Terror*, London: Ashgate, 2005.

Chapter 2 Continuity and Change

1.   Peter Hall, *Cities of Tomorrow. An Intellectual History of Urban Planning and Design in the Twentieth Century*, Oxford: Blackwell, updated edition, 1996, p. 399.

2.   Anthony Dyson, Review of *Faith in the City*, *Theology*, LXXXIX/732, London: SPCK, 1986, p. 486.

3.   Adrian Hastings, *A History of English Christianity*, London: SCM Press, fourth edn, 2001, p. xxxviii.

4.   Archbishop's Commission on Urban Priority Areas, *Faith in the City: A Call for Action by Church and Nation*, London: Church House Publishing, 1985, p. xiv.

5.   *Faith in the City*, p. 360.

6.   Richard Wilkinson, *The Impact of Inequality*, London: Routledge, 2005.

7.   Mervyn King, Deputy Governor of the Bank of England, Speech to the Black Country Consortium at Molineux, Wolverhampton on Monterary Policy and Manufacturing Industry, 29 March 2000.

8.   However, access to airports for international visitors and business clients tend to take priority over public transport systems for ordinary residents.

9.   *Our Towns and Cities – The Future, Delivering an Urban Renaissance*, ODPM/the Stationery Office, 2000,

10. Ben Jupp, *Keeping the Faiths: The New Covenant between Religious Belief and Secular Power*, Demos Collection 11, 2000

11. Robert Putnam, *Bowling Alone: The Collapse and Revival of American Community*, London: Simon & Schuster, 2000.

12. *Faithful Regeneration: The Role and Contribution of Local Parishes in Local Communities in the Diocese of Birmingham*: http://www.active-citizen.org.uk/files/downloads/Reports/Faithful%20Regeneration.pdf.

13. Robert Furbey and Marie Macey, 'Religion and Urban Regeneration: A Place for Faith?' *Policy and Politics*, Vol. 33, No. 1, 2005, pp. 95-116.

14. National Secular Society: http://secularism.org.uk/index.php?option=contents&task=view&id=129&itemid=35.

15. See Laurie Green, *Let's Do Theology*, London: Geoffrey Chapman, 1990; Elaine Graham, Heather Walton and Frances Ward, *Theological Reflection: Methods*, London: SCM Press, 2005; Robert Schreiter, Constructing Local Theologies, New York: Orbis, 1985.

16. General Synod debate on the Church Urban Fund, July 1995.

17. Jeff Astley, *Ordinary Theology: Looking Listening and Learning in Theology*, London: Ashgate, 2002.

18. Robert Beckford, *Jesus is Dread*, London: Darton, Longman & Todd, 1998, Anthony Reddie, *Nobodies to Somebodies: A Practical Theology for Education and Liberation*, London: Epworth, 2003.

19. In other words, while we are witnessing the end of the cultural, political and intellectual predominance of Western Christianity – the death of 'Christendom' – neither have the predictions of the so-called 'secularization thesis', forecasting the ultimate disappearance of religious faith altogether, entirely come to pass.

Chapter 3 The World in Our Churches: Diversity and Difference

1.   The *Guardian*, 21 January 2005 – G2 section.

2.   The *Guardian*, 23 January 2006.

3.   The *Guardian*, 21 January 2005 – G2 section.

4.   A careful and developed exploration of the idea of 'diversity' and its various forms is presented in B. Parekh, *Rethinking Multiculturalism: Cultural Diversity and Political Theory*, second edition, London: Palgrave Macmillan, 2005.

5.   *Presence and Engagement* – report presented to the General Synod of the Church of England by the Inter Faith Consultative Group, Mission and Public Affairs Division, Archbishops' Council, July 2005.

6.   K. Leech, *Race: Changing Society and the Churches*, London: SPCK, 2005, pp. 49–50.

7.   E. Soja, 'Postmodern Urbanization: The Six Restructurings of Los Angeles' in S. Watson and K. Gibson (eds), *Postmodern Cities and Spaces*, Oxford: Blackwell, 1995.

8.   R. Sennett, *The Corrosion of Character: The Personal Consequences of Work in the New Capitalism*, London: W.W. Norton and Company, 1998.

9.   D.A. Held, A. McGrew, D. Goldblatt and J. Perraton, *Global Transformations: Politics, Economics and Culture*, Cambridge: Polity Press, 1999, p. 283, quoted in D. Thorns, *The Transformation of Cities: Urban Theory and Urban Life*, London: Palgrave Macmillan, 2002, p. 58.

10.   http://www.mtv.co.uk/

11.   http://www.mobo.com/index.html

12.   http://www.ukgospel.com/

13.   Fred Lynch, Youth Specialties Youth Work Conference, Seminar 'Understanding Hip-Hop Culture', Pittsburgh PA, October 2005.

14.   Z. Bauman, *Identity*, Cambridge: Polity Press, 2004, p. 46.

15.   *Spiritual Health and the Well-Being of Urban Young People*, London: Commission on Urban Life and Faith. For the full report see the Commission's website: http://www.culf.org.uk

16.   G. Lemos, *The Search for Tolerance: Challenging and Changing Racist Attitudes and Behaviour Amongst Young People*, York: Joseph Rowntree Foundation, 2005.

17.   *Home Office, Statistics on Race and the Criminal Justice System*, London: Home Office, 2004, p. vii.

18.   The research on Spiritual health and the well-being of urban young people requested by the Commission suggests that young people who express a faith commitment are significantly more prone to bullying at school.

19.   Runnymede Trust, *Islamophobia: A Challenge for Us All*, London: Runnymede Trust, 1997.

20.   J. Nielsen and C. Allen, *Anti-Islamic reactions within the European Union after the Recent Acts of Terror against the USA*, European Monitoring Centre on Racism and Xenophobia, October 2001.

21.   British National Party website: http://www.bnp.org.uk – last visited 21 December 2005.

22.   P. Dwyer, *Understanding Social Citizenship: Themes and Perspectives for Policy and Practice*, Bristol: The Policy Press, 2004.

23.   SEU (Social Exclusion Unit), *Minority Ethnic Issues in Social Exclusion and Neighbourhood Renewal*, London: Cabinet Office, p.17.

24.   An asylum seeker is 'someone who is fleeing persecution, has arrived in another country, made themselves known to the authorities and exercised a right to apply for asylum'. A refugee is 'someone whose asylum application has been turned down and is awaiting a return to their country. If it is not safe for failed asylum seekers to return, they may have to stay for the time being'. Refugee Council, *Press Myths*, London: The Refugee Council, 2005 – www.refugeecouncil.org.uk

25.   Refugee Council, *Tell it Like it Is: The Truth About Asylum*, London: The Refugee Council, 2005 – www.refugeecouncil.org.uk

26.   Duncan Forrester, *Apocalypse Now?: Reflections on Faith in a Time of Terror*, London: Ashgate 2005.

27.   M. Ruthven, *Fundamentalism: The Search for Meaning*, Oxford: Oxford University Press, 2004, p. 8.

28.   R. Harries, *God Outside the Box: Why Spiritual People Object to Christianity*, London, SPCK, 2002, p.78.

29.   Leaflet published by the Churches' Commission for Racial Justice: A Commission of Churches Together in Britain and Ireland, 2004.

30.   Presentation to a conference on 'Counteracting political extremism (BNP): the role of the local church'; convened by the Commission on Urban Life and Faith, at the Parish Church of St John and St Peter, Ladywood, Birmingham, 27 February 2005.

31.   Church Action on Poverty, 2005; www.church-poverty.org.uk

32.   Francis Davis, Von Hugel Institute, St Edmunds College, Cambridge.

33.   A. Gilchrist, *The Well-Connected Community: A Networking Approach to Community Development*, Bristol: The Policy Press, 2004, p. 6.

34. K. Leech, *Race: Changing Society and the Churches*, London: SPCK, 2005, pp. 76-7. See also Nicholas Holtam and Sue Mayo, *Learning from the Conflict. Reflections on the Struggle against the British National Party on the Isle of Dogs*, London: Jubilee Group, 1998.

35. Contribution by Nicholas Holtam to a conference on 'Counteracting political extremism (BNP): the role of the local church'; convened by the Commission on Urban Life and Faith, at the Parish Church of St John and St Peter, Ladywood, Birmingham, 27 February 2005.

36. Professor Sir Bernard Crick, a Vice-President of the British Humanist Association, has argued for collaboration with people of faith that he identifies as sharing common ground. See B. Crick, 'This age of fanaticism is no time for non-believers to make enemies', The *Guardian*, 20 October 2005.

37. R. Furbey, A. Dinham, R. Farnell, D. Finneron with G. Wilkinson, C. Howarth, D. Hussain and S. Palmer , *Faith as Social Capital: Connecting or Dividing?*, Bristol: The Policy Press, 2006.

38. Diocese of Leicester, Leicester Council of Faiths, and Voluntary Action Leicester, *Embracing the Present, Planning the Future: Social Action by the Faith Communities of Leicester*, Leicester: Diocese of Leicester - July 2004.

Chapter 4 Prosperity: In Pursuit of Well-being

1. http://www.hm-treasury.gov.uk/media/FA6/29/pbro5_chapter4_130.pdf

2. The research of one such modest unit, the William Temple Foundation, which is promoting the development of religious capital, and its contribution to debates over social capital, happiness, and life satisfaction, are central to this chapter.

3. Income inequality is measured by the Gini coefficient. The Gini coefficient takes values between 0 and 100, and the lower the value, the more equally household income is distributed. For more detail, see www.statistics.gov.uk.

4. Sources: Office for National Statistics; Institute for Fiscal Studies; http://www.statistics.gov.uk/CCI/nugget.asp?ID=332&Pos=&ColRank=1&Rank=192

5. *Poverty and inequality in Britain*: 2005 IFS.

6. Pre-budget report, December 2005, HM Treasury, Cm 6701.

7. *Income Wealth and Inequalities*, House of Commons Library, research paper 04/70; 15 September 2004.

8. A good starting place in reading up on this issue is Professor Wilkinson's ground-breaking book *Unhealthy Societies - The Afflictions of Inequality*, London: Routledge, 1996.

9. Sue Regan and Peter Robinson in *Overcoming Disadvantage: An Agenda for the Next 20 Years*, York: Joseph Rowntree Foundation, 2004, p. 14.

10. We use the term secular capitalism to distinguish between the current narrow value base of capitalism (power, profit and status) in comparison to the earlier forms of capitalism and its association with responsibility for the well-being of the less fortunate.

11. Ruth Lister, *Poverty*, Bristol: The Polity Press, 2004.

12. Polly Toynbee, *Hard Work, Life in Low Paid Britain*, London: Bloomsbury, 2003, p. 239.

13. *Poverty and the Political Economy of Prosperity*, January 2005.

14. P. Jones, 'Access to Credit on a Low income' in *How People on Low Incomes Manage Their Finances*, Economic and Social Research Council, 2001.

15. Ruth Lister, *Poverty* (see n. 10 above).

16. Ruth Lister, The *Guardian*, November 2004.

17. *Listen Hear, Report of Commission on Poverty, Participation and Power*, January 2001, http://www.oxfamgb.org/ukpp/resources/listenhear_summary.htm

18. Church Action on Poverty, *Speaking from Experience, Voices at the National Poverty Hearing*, 1996, p. 30.

19. See DFID Sustainable Livelihoods Guidance Sheets at www.livelihoods.org for further information on the concept, framework and uses of the approach.

20. UNDP, Governance for Sustainable Livelihoods, 1998 p. 7.

21. C. Rakodi, Urban livelihoods: A People-centred Approach to Reducing Poverty, Earthscan, 2002.

22. For more see www/lnweb18.worldbank.org

23. Richard Layard, Lionel Robbins Memorial Lectures, 2002/03; http://cep.lse.ac.uk/layard/

24. *Households below Average Income: An Analysis of the Income Distribution 1994-95 to 2003-04*, Department of Works and Pensions (DWP), 2005.

25. *Spiritual Health and the Well-being of Urban Young People*: available at www.culf.org.uk

26. Percentages add up to more than 100% because young people were asked separate questions about how likely they would be to approach each person for help. Some young people would consider approaching more than one of the people listed.

27. Source: Survey of the mental health of children and young people in Great Britain, 2004.

28. Source: 2001/02 British Crime Survey, Home Office.

29. Sources: General Household Survey, Office for National Statistics for drinking data.

30. Sources: Survey of smoking, drinking and drug use among young people in England, Department of Health General Household Survey, Office for National Statistics (published January 2006).

31. http://www.euro.who.int/mediacentre/PR/2004/20040603_1

32. Rowan Williams, 'Who's bringing up our children?', Citizens Organizing Foundation lecture, Queen Mary College, University of London, 11 April 2005.

33. See further details of research on http://culf.org/papers/uypbriefing.pdf

34. Author of authentic happiness and the Fox Leadership Professor of Psychology at the University of Pennsylvania.

35. For further information see New Economics Foundation website www.neweconomics.org

36. http://www.neweconomics.org/gen/hottopics_well-being.aspx

37. T. Jackson, F. Laing, A. MacGillivray, N. Marks, J. Ralls and S. Stymne, *An Index of Sustainable Economic Welfare for the UK 1950–1996*. Centre for Environmental Strategy, University of Surrey, 1997.

38. Local quality of life indicators – supporting communities to become sustainable: www.audit-commission.gov.uk

Chapter 5 Regeneration for People: More than Status, Power and Profit

1. K. Klunzman, *Regeneration and Renewal*, 19 November 2004.

2. http://www.powerinquiry.org/publications/index.php

3. Neil Smith 'New Globalism, New Urbanism: Gentrification as Global Urban Strategy' in *Antipode*, Vol. 34, Issue 3, July.

4. Tim Butler, *London Calling*, Berg, 2002.

5. This is for historic reasons connected to the contraction of manufacturing and heavy industry which was often close to the waterways.

6. *The Waternet: A Blueprint for Modal Shift and Sustainable Development*, report by Jonathan Rosenberg, 2002.

7. Oral evidence to the ODPM: Housing, Planning Local Government and the Regions Committee, 28 October 2002.

8. R. Dorey, *Churches on the Edge: The North Southwark Experience of Government Policies, 2005*: www.st-edmunds.cam.ac.uk/vhi/fis/fpr/dorey.pdf

9. www.cof.org.uk

10. www.wtf.org.uk/core_cities_network.htm

11. Walter Brueggemann, *The Prophetic Imagination*, Minneapolis: Fortress Press, 2001.

12. See, for example, Helen Cameron, Douglas Davies, Philip Richter and Frances Ward (eds), Studying Local Churches, London: SCM Press, 2005.

13. http://www.operation-eden.org.uk/

14. Peter Marcuse, 'The "War on Terrorism" and Life in Cities after September 11, 2001' in Stephen Graham, *Cities, War and Terrorism*, Oxford: Blackwell, 2004

15. www.faithworks.info/

16. Rowan Williams, *Writing in the Dust*, London: Hodder & Stoughton, 2002, p. 61.

17. Luke Bretherton, *A New Establishment? Theological Politics and the Emerging Church/State Relations*, King's College London, 2005.

18. Brendan Martin, 'What is Public about Public Services?', London: Public World, 2004.

19. CBI unit on public service reform. http://www.cbi.org.uk/ndbs/staticpages.nsf/StaticPages/home.html/?OpenDocument

20. The Rt Hon. David Blunkett MP, when Home Secretary, Edith Kahn Memorial Lecture, June 2003.

21. Fred Rattley, Community Regeneration Department, Diocese of Birmingham, visit by Commissioners to Birmingham, January 2005.

22. R. Dorey, *Churches on the Edge: The North Southwark Experience of Government Policies, 2005*: www.st-edmunds.cam.ac.uk/vhi/fis/fpr/dorey.pdf

23. Wythenshawe Family Support Co-ordinator, Shrewsbury Diocese Catholic Children's Society.

24. Sermon for the Southwark Diocese Centenary, July 2005.

Chapter 6 A Good City: Urban Regeneration with People in Mind

1. Leonie Sandercock, *Cosmopolis II: Mongrel Cities*, London: Continuum, 2003.

2. Peter Scott, *A Political Theology of Nature*, Cambridge: Cambridge University Press, 2003; Peter

Scott, 'A Eucharistic Theology of Place' in C. Bartholomew and F. Hughes (eds), *Explorations in a Christian Theology of Pilgrimage*, London: Ashgate, 2004, pp. 151-69.

3.   See www.greatbuildings.com/architects/Le_Corbusier.html for examples.

4.   Doreen Massey, 'Living in Wythenshawe' in Ian Borden, Joe Kerr, Jane Refill with Alicia Pivaro (eds), *The Unknown City. Contesting Architecture and Social Space*, The MIT Press, 2001.

5.   David Harvey, *Justice, Nature and the Geography of Difference*, Oxford: Blackwell, 1996.

6.   Peter Scott, *A Political Theology of Nature* (see n. 2 above).

7.   Timothy Gorringe, *A Theology of the Built Environment: Justice, Empowerment, Redemption*, Cambridge: Cambridge University Press, 2003.

8.   http://www.odpm.gov.uk/pub/302/Summit2005ReportbackPDF905Kb_id1140302.pdf

9.   http://www.ohchr.org/english/law/millennium.htm

10.   Timothy Gorringe, *A Theology of the Built Environment* (see n. 7 above).

11.   *Our Cities Are Back: Competitive Cities Make Prosperous Regions and Sustainable Communities* HMT/ODPM/DTI: http://www.odpm.gov.uk/pub/455/OurcitiesarebackPDF1396Kb_id1127455.pdf

12.   David Harvey, *Justice, Nature and the Geography of Difference*, Oxford: Blackwell, 1996.

13.   Peter Scott 'A Eucharistic Theology of Place' in C. Bartholomew and F. Hughes (eds), *Explorations in a Christian Theology of Pilgrimage*, London: Ashgate, 2004, pp. 151-69.

14.   Frank Field, *Neighbours from Hell - The Politics of Behaviour*, London: Politicos, 2003.

15.   For more information see www.streetpastors.org.uk

16.   http://www.urbantaskforce.org/UTF_final_report.pdf

17.   Leonie Sandercock, *Cosmopolis II: Mongrel Cities* (see n. 1 above).

18.   Ash Amin, Doreen Massey and Nigel Thrift, *Cities for the Many not for the Few*, Bristol: Policy Press 2001.

19.   http://www.methodist.org.uk/downloads/ne_gambcasinoconsultation_1005.doc

20.   Samuel Ferguson Lecture, Manchester 2005.

21.   www.cottingleycornerstone.org.uk

22.   Steven Graham, Cities, War and Terrorism, Oxford: Blackwell, 2004.

23.   Lines from "Dreams Before Waking' *Your Native Land, Your Life:* Poems by Adrienne Rich. Copyright © 1986 by Adrienne Rich. Used by permission of the author and W. W. Norton & Company Inc.

Chapter 7 Involved and Committed

1.   Bridge Builders Preston: an interfaith research project funded for 12 months by M. B. Reckitt Trust until March 2006. Aiming to increase capacity of religious organizations to engage in partnerships in regeneration and service provision. Further information available at: http://mysite.wanadoo-members.co.uk/credoconsultancy/bridgebuilderspreston.htm [accessed 02/02/06]

2.   http://communities.homeoffice.gov.uk/raceandfaith/reports_pubs/publications/race_faith/workingtog_faith.pdf

3.   Rowan Williams in his presidential address to the General Synod in York on Monday 11 July 2005.

4.   Bishop John Sentamu's foreword to 'A Call for the Continued Growth of Effective Joint Working in Birmingham' by the Flourishing Neighbourhoods Group, published by the Diocese of Birmingham in 2005.

5.   S. Wells, *Community-Led Regeneration and the Local Church*, Cambridge: Grove Booklets (P94), 2003.

6.   'Angels and Advocates', Churches Regional Commission for Yorkshire and the Humber.

7.   Richard Farnell, Robert Furbey, Stephen Shams al Haqq Hills, Marie Macey and Greg Smith, *'Faith' in Urban Regeneration? Engaging Faith Communities in Urban Regeneration*, Bristol: The Policy Press 2003.

Chapter 8 Grounding and Sustaining Faithful Capital

1.   Tony Blair addressing church leaders and representatives of other faiths at a Faithworks lecture, March 2005.

2.   *Faith in England's Northwest: Economic Impact Assessment*, February 2005. This report follows up previous research The Contribution made by Faith Communities to Civil society in the Region, November 2003.

3.   See Church Life Profile 2001, Churches Information for Mission.

4.   2003 Home Office Citizenship Survey: People, Families and Communities.

5.   *Church Statistics 2003/4:* http://www.cofe.anglican.org/info/statistics/index.html

6.   Building Faith in Our Future: Report of the Church Heritage Forum, London: Church House Publishing, 2004.

7. Opinion Research National Polls 2005, 2003, 2001 for the Archbishops' Council: http://www.cofe.anglican.org/info/statistics

8. While 86% had been inside a church building in the previous 12 months, only 48% had been to a library, 46% had been to a historic house/garden and 51% had been to the cinema – Opinion Research Business (ORB) Survey, October 2003.

9. 86% of adults in Britain had been into a church or place of worship in the previous year – including 89% of Christians, 75% of those of other faiths and 80% of those who said they had nor religion – Opinion Research Business (ORB) Survey, October 2003. (For more see Building Faith in Our Future, London: Church House Publishing, 2004.)

10. http://www.cofe.anglican.org/info/statistics/orb2005churchfunding.pdf

11. The Community Interest Company (CIC) is a type of company designed for Social Enterprises that want to use their profits and assets for the public good (www.dti.gov.uk/cics/).

12. Opinion Research National Polls 2005, 2003, 2001 for the Archbishops' Council: http://www.cofe.anglican.org/info/statistics

13. The term 'patient attention' was used by Dr Rowan Williams in his presidential address to the General Synod in York on Monday 11 July 2005.

14. See www.alm.org.uk/city/outreach/index.php

15. James Q. Wilson and Jonathan Sacks, The Moral Sense, London: The Smith Institute, 2002, p. 15.

16. Adapted from Mike Frost's paper 'Church in Missional Mode', for more see www.biblesociety.org.uk/exploratory/articles/frost01.doc

17. These include the Eden Project (www.message.org.uk) and Urban Presence (www.urbanpresence.org.uk) in Manchester; the Order of Mission associated with St Thomas, Crookes in Sheffield (www.sttoms.net); Urban Expression in London and Glasgow (www.urbanexpression.org.uk); and The Regeneration Trust in Tollerton, North London (regenerationtrust.org).

18. The Bridge, Newspaper of the Anglican Diocese of Southwark, Vol. 10, No. 9, November 2005.

19. Presence and Engagement: The Churches' Task in a Multi Faith Society, Report by the Mission and Public Affairs Council, GS 1577, p. 13 para. 28.

20. http://schoolofurbanmission.org/
    http://www.intercivilization.net/
    http://www.message.org.uk/projects.cfm?id=24
    http://www.utusheffield.fsnet.co.uk/
    http://www.urbanpresence.org.uk/pages/upframe.html

21. Formation for Ministry within a Learning Church: The Structure and Funding of Ordination Training (The Hind Report) GS 1496, General Synod 2003. This report heralded the debate on developments in theological training associated with ordained ministry, in particular, ecumenical Regional Training Partnerships which are due to come on stream over the next five years.

22. This approach was suggested by Dr Howard Worsley of St John's College, Nottingham. See www.ascd.org/portal/site/ascd for a description of this approach.

23. For more information see www.umtp.org/html/home.html

24. Faith in the City, §6.57, p. 119.

25. See http://www.supplementaryschools.org.uk/site/

Photo credits

Unless stated specifically in the list below all images are courtesy of the Ingram Publishing Image Library ©.

Main cover photo: F8-infinity photography © 2005
Inset cover images left to right:
    © Photodics Inc
    © Ingram Publishing image library.
    © Joy Douglas
    © Photodics Inc.

Back cover inset images
left to right
    © Joy Douglas
    © Andy Stonehouse 2005
    © David Johnston 2004

p iv	Top: Croydon market © Andy Stonehouse 2006
	Bottom: Kathleen Richardson, Source unknown
p 1	London Eye © Andy Stonehouse 2006
p 2	Candle light vigil © Andy Stonehouse 2005
p 3	York © Mark Sheppard 2004
p 4	Bottom: © Andy Stonehouse 2006
p 5	Top: Akasah community temple © Andy Stonehouse 2006
	Middle: Synagogue © Andy Stonehouse 2006
	Bottom: © Comstock Image library
p 6	Outside the Islam Centre, Tooting © Andy Stonehouse 2006
p 10	Bottom: Gas Street Basin, Birmingham © Andy Stonehouse 2004
p 12	Both images: The Thornbury Centre, Bradford © David Johnston 2004
p 16	Both images: © Andy Stonehouse 2006
p 17	© Joy Douglas
p 18	Top: © Photodisc Image library
	Bottom: © Andy Stonehouse 2006
p 19	© Andy Stonehouse 2006
p 20	© Imagesource photo library
p 21	Top: © Andy Stonehouse 2006
p 23	Bottom: © Joy Douglas
p 25	© Andy Stonehouse 2006
p 26	© Andy Stonehouse 2006
p 27	Bottom: © Imagesource photo library
p 28	© Imagesource photo library
p 30	Top: © Photodisc Image library
	Bottom: © Andy Stonehouse 2006
p 32	Fern Lodge Estate © Andy Stonehouse 2006
p 33	Top: © Andy Stonehouse 2006
	Bottom: © Pamela Wise
p 34	Top: © AP Davey
p 36	© Comstock Image library
p 37	© Stockbyte Image library

p 38   © Rubber Ball image library

p 40   Both images: © Imagesource photo library

p 41   Bottom: © Imagesource photo library

p 45   © Photodisc Image library

p 50   © Andy Stonehouse 2006

p 51   © Andy Stonehouse 2004

p 52   Bullring, Birmingham © F8-infinity photography 2005

p 55   Top: © Andy Stonehouse 2005

        Bottom: © AP Davey

p 56   Top: © Stockbyte Image library

        Bottom:© Andy Stonehouse 2004

p 57   © Andy Stonehouse 2005

p 58   © Photodisc Image library

p 59   Bottom: © AP Davey

p 60   Top: © Andy Stonehouse 2006

        Bottom: © Joy Douglas

p 61   Top: © Stockbyte Image library

p 62   © Lewisham Street Pastors

p 63   Top: © IMS Communications Ltd

p 64   Top: © Joy Douglas

p 69   Birmingham © Andy Stonehouse 2005

p 71   Top: © London Citizens

p 74   Top: © Photodisc Image library

p 75   © Andy Stonehouse 2005

p 76   Top: © BrandX picture library

        Bottom: © Photodisc Image library

p77   © Chris Epsom

p 78   Top: Wedding, Richmond © Andy Stonehouse 2004

        Bottom: St Matthew's, Brixton © Andy Stonehouse 2004

p 79   Bottom: © Joy Douglas

p 81   © Marcus Perkins 2004

p 83   Anita Roddick, Greenbelt '04 © Andy Stonehouse 2004

p 85   Bottom: © AP Davey

p 88   Top: © Photodisc Image library

        Bottom: © Andy Stonehouse 2006

p 91   Top: © Stockbyte Image library

Acknowledgements

The Commission on Urban Life and Faith was the initiative of the Church of England through its Archbishops.

Membership

The Commission consisted of 8 members of the Church of England, 2 Roman Catholics, 1 member of the United Reformed Church, 1 Methodist and 1 Muslim and was representative of age, gender and ethnic background. The members were:

Graham Cook, URC, Merseyside

Rob Furbey, Sheffield Hallam University

Tim Gardam, St Anne's College, Oxford

Elaine Graham, Manchester University

Catherine Howarth, London Citizens

Dilwar Hussain, Islamic Foundation, Leicester

Pamela Ingham, Priest, Newcastle

Bernard Longley, Roman Catholic Auxiliary Bishop in Westminster

Stephen Lowe, Bishop of Hulme

Sharon Palmer, Researcher and Adviser, Birmingham

Dean Pusey, Youth Officer, Southwark Diocese

Kathleen Richardson (Chair), Methodist Minister

John Sentamu (Vice-Chair), Archbishop of York

Ann Morisy, Helen Patterson (seconded by HM Treasury) and Alison Cundiff provided the Secretariat.

Fran Beckett (Chief Executive of the Church Urban Fund), Andrew Davey (Urban Officer for the Church of England) and Rabbi Jason Kleiman acted as consultants.

Malcolm Doney and Martin Wroe acted as editorial consultants.

Additional material in the Report was provided by John Atherton, Niall Cooper and Chris Baker.

The Commission was given office accommodation within Church House, Westminster.

The Church Urban Fund gave a significant grant. Further grants for specific pieces of research were received from the Tudor Trust, the Wates Foundation, and the Westhill Foundation.

Terms of reference

The terms of reference given to the Commission were:

1. To examine and evaluate progress made by both Church and Nation in improving the life of those living in urban areas;
2. To identify and articulate the significant changes in urban communities that have resulted from deindustrialization, population movements and the impact of globalization;
3. To reflect on the challenge which God may be making to the Church and nation;
4. To offer a vision of urban society, and the Church's presence and witness within it at the beginning of the twenty-first century;
5. To make recommendations to the appropriate bodies.

Purpose

We further identified our purpose as:

To promote a vision of urban life which analyses and addresses the realities of its glories, injustices and needs.

As always in a Commission, the work fell unevenly over the members and some were able to give significantly more time and energy to the writing of the Report. But all participated through their expertise and different gifts and the experience has been stimulating and fulfilling, if at times taxing and occasionally painful.

We want to acknowledge the work that is being done in urban settings by people, to whom we express our thanks for their generous hospitality, and the way they shared with us the faith, creativity and imagination they demonstrate in serving their local communities.

The report could have been longer and much interesting material has had to be omitted. Some of this can be seen on the Commission's web site at: www.culf.org.uk